Art Place Japan

The Echigo-Tsumari Art Triennale and the Vision to Reconnect Art and Nature

Fram Kitagawa

Translated by Amiko Matsuo and Brad Monsma
with essays by Lynne Breslin and Adrian Favell

Princeton Architectural Press, New York

Contents

The Echigo-Tsumari Art Triennale: How It All Began

Every three years since its inauguration in 2000, the Echigo-Tsumari Art Triennale has brought together art, ecology, and communities in the Echigo-Tusmari region of Niigata Prefecture, Japan. Each edition results in a large number of site-specific works of art installed in rice fields and empty farmhouses and schools in the *satoyama* landscape, as the region's border zone landscape of cultivated, arable land between forested mountains is called. The first festival invited artists from thirty-two countries and featured 148 projects; the second hosted twenty-three countries and featured 158 projects; the third, forty and 225; the fourth, twenty-seven and 228; the fifth, twenty-nine and 175; and the sixth, seventeen and 180.

The projects are always dispersed throughout the region. This land of nearly three hundred square miles is historically known for the heavy snowfall that, before snowplows existed, each winter isolated its more than two hundred communities from each other. However, the communities thrived by supporting one another, collectively overcoming the challenges of living in snow country. The Echigo-Tsumari region encompasses all of these distinctive communities, each with its own set of local cultural codes, and through the triennial we want viewers to experience the full historicity and cultural context of the area. The involvement of the communities in the triennial has grown from 2 in the first edition to 38 in the second, 67 in the third, 92 in the fourth, and 102 in the fifth, showing the slow but growing acceptance of the festival.

When a magnitude-six earthquake struck in Nagano Prefecture on March 12, 2011, it was felt strongly in the region where the Echigo-Tsumari Art Triennale is held. It took place the day after the Tōhoku earthquake and tsunami and thus did not receive a lot of media coverage, but many people were injured and numerous properties were destroyed. The devastating effects of the earthquake threatened the possibility of the fifth edition of the triennial the following year. But the local residents did not sit back to await handouts, donations, and government support. They felt strongly that they wanted to work hard, using their own strength, to rebuild in time for the next festival.

In response to the attitude of the communities, I felt a strong sense that we had better address the damage caused by the earthquake quickly and have a spectacular fifth edition. My sentiments were mirrored by the other triennial organizers and officials. But I was in fact initially puzzled by this response of the people of Echigo-Tsumari, given that they had been so ambivalent, even oppositional, toward the triennial at first. I realized with much gratification that they had come to take great pride in the art festival and felt toward it a sense of ownership. I became newly appreciative of the local identity of Echigo-Tsumari and the growing sense of dignity that its people were perceiving as a direct and indirect result of our activities there since 2000. This was a defining moment for me, confirming my motivations for having sustained the triennial for so long.

The Echigo-Tsumari Art Triennale was originally conceived for the purpose of revitalizing the region, which suffered from depopulation and an aging population. In the 1950s, Japan's younger generations began leaving the rural areas of the country in greater and greater numbers to work in the cities, which the remaining communities of farmers, particularly in Japan's mountainous snow country, felt as a strong blow. In subsequent decades the government even ordered that the remaining members of rural communities stop farming too and move to the cities, where their work and lives could be more efficiently managed. These shortsighted and imbalanced policies of prioritizing the urban over the rural not only fatally weakened the country, but also robbed elderly farmers of their dignity and purpose in life. Their agricultural work was an important part of their identity, and being stripped of it— which was to deny their years spent cultivating and learning the skills of the trade, living with nature, and creating a way of life—was devastating. I imagine the elders' sense of loss, seeing their hometowns and ancestral gravesites disappearing, fearing that their children would not return again until their funerals. Many buildings that had once been beautiful and sturdy, made from magnificent cedars, their walls perfectly smooth, were now deserted and decaying. There was emptiness where there had once been laughter, tears, arguments, and fun.

The Echigo-Tsumari Art Triennale was conceived as something positive and memorable for the elderly residents who remain in the region. The artists taking place in the festival want to commemorate through their work here the decline of the population, the abandoned homes and schools. Since its beginning in 2000, the hundreds of artworks made for the triennial have acknowledged the pride that residents of this region still take in their work and way of life. At a time when efficiency and the lowest common denominator have become the norm, art—a close friend to humans across the world since ancient times—can challenge those paradigms by placing importance on how different each individual person is.

Revitalizing Rural Communities: The New Niigata Risou Plan

In the late 1990s, the Japanese government launched a variety of initiatives concerning local community development. Community building, regional redevelopment, and provincial revitalization were conceived as strategies for the centralization of local communities, and participation therein was symbolic of support for larger merger policies that were being undertaken on a national scale at the same time.

As part of these policies, Niigata Prefecture launched the New Niigata Risou Plan in 1994, which stated that the prefecture would assume 60 percent of the total costs for new projects dedicated to developing local regional identities and involving the participation of the residents. Rather than emphasizing infrastructure by constructing new buildings, the decision was made to invest in human capital.

The prefecture's major cities, Tokamachi City and Tsunan Town, dedicated themselves to finding a way to survive the challenging circumstances that were causing so many of their residents to move to Tokyo, such as the decline of the textile and farming industries and an aging population. Various dubious proposals were put forth: for a Leonardo da Vinci Museum, botanical gardens, or converting a closed schoolhouse to a manga museum. But most of these proposals were not truly sustainable strategies.

Considerable criticism surrounding these initiatives intensified in 1995. Tokamachi City was deeply interested in creating its own version of the Risou Plan that would place a strong priority on human capital and regional development. I was invited, at this point, to be part of the steering committee, partly because of my previous involvement with Faret Tachikawa, a public art project for urban redevelopment in Tokyo.

The Echigo-Tsumari Art Necklace

Could art be a strategy for redeveloping the region? Could using public spaces for art be a way of pushing the idea of art beyond museums? These were the questions the people from the prefecture posed to me. But how to take it from there? The answer: with considerable quarreling about everything.

We tried organizing study sessions hosted by prominent members of each municipality but could never get beyond deciding on a nickname for the project before a dispute would break out. If we used Tokamachi in the name, the other municipalities would oppose. Eventually, I proposed using the traditional place name of Echigo-sho (encompassing the towns of Tokamachi, Tsunan, Kawanishi, and Nakasato) and Matsunoyama-go (Matsudai and Matsunoyama), and incorporating "Tsumari," which resulted in Echigo-Tsumari, and people were appeased. We developed the idea of the "Echigo-Tsumari Art Necklace Project," which would be based on three major pillars.

The first of the three pillars was a competition called "80,000 Residents Discover Something Unique about Echigo-Tsumari." Residents of the region, as well as visitors, were encouraged to discover and establish the characteristics of the place. We held writing and photography contests to capture the local charm and focus attention on the richness of the region's nature and culture. The 3,114 entries were reviewed by a team of jurors, including the poet Makoto Ooka, the actress Kyoko Maya, the photographer Shigeo Anzai, and the designer Daisuke Nakatsuka. The project resulted in a vivid depiction of the local lifeways over the course of the four seasons, from the heavy wintertime snowfall to the terraced rice fields and their summertime yields.

The second pillar was "The Way of Flowers." This project was a joint venture involving community participation. Elderly gardeners played a central role in connecting the municipal districts by planting flowers alongside roads and in the front gardens of the traditional Japanese houses of the region. This was intended to build networks among the communities through the familiar guise of flowers. This project expanded to include infrastructure development, such as construction of roads and park buildings.

The third pillar was titled "Stage Construction." Each of the region's six municipalities was asked to establish and maintain a strategic foothold, by which was meant an institutional base, or stage, that would serve as a kind of showroom embodying characteristics of the region. (An earlier example of showcasing regions in Japan was the Michi no Eki, or Roadside Station program, established in the early 1990s. This was, however, shortsighted in that it only focused on selling products; our "stages" were developed as something entirely different.

The following were the initial concepts for the region's stages:

- The Tokamachi City stage would be referred to as the "Echigo-Tsumari Market" and would serve as an invigorating place for cultural exchange.
- The Kawanishi stage would be a "New Agri-Garden City Development," a twenty-first-century proposal for living in a new kind of garden city while at the same time referring to the region's history of agriculture.
- The Nakasato stage would be called "The Shinano River Story," and its themes would be the lives of the three million people living in the Shinano River basin and the rehabilitation of those communities.
- The Tsunan stage, "Jomon and Play," would be focused on the ancient flame-type ceramics produced by the Neolithic Jomon culture that were unearthed in Tsunan Town. The goal was to create a space where one could experience a connection with nature.

- The Matsudai stage, "Snow-Land Agrarian Culture," would represent the variety of perspectives and wisdom embedded in local lifeways and build pride in them.
- The Matsunoyama stage, "The School of Forest," would reach beyond local concerns to regenerate *satoyama*.

Eventually, Matsunoyama founded the Echigo-Matsunoyama Museum of Natural Science, Kyororo, based on the idea that "every resident is a scientist," which served to help the museum become well rooted within the community.

Matsudai built the Matsudai Snow-Land Agrarian Culture Center NOHBUTAI, which became the center of activities and staff for the triennial.

The Echigo-Tsumari Exchange Center KINARE in Tokamachi was one of the first stages to be realized. It was intended to be a center for traditional crafts, such as kimonos and textiles. In 2012 it was transformed into the Echigo-Tsumari Satoyama Museum of Contemporary Art.

Kawanishi tried to work with the architect Paolo Soleri to produce an ecological concept through architecture, but was ultimately frustrated by the results. Tsunan independently created a facility only focused on Jomon culture. Nakasato was unable to create its stage, and the regional offices there continue to suffer from not having been able to establish an institution.

The Echigo-Tsumari Art Triennale has served, in part, to create a network out of these pillars and activities. Once the stages were established, the responsibility to develop goals for cultural sustainability increased. In other words, these stages and artworks needed to be protected and sustained beyond the ephemeral festivities that happened only every three years. As business ventures, they are required to become economically sustainable.

Conception and Background of the Triennial

Echigo-Tsumari is in the southern part of Niigata Prefecture, which is mountainous and hilly and has very little flat arable land. Our first investigation into possible sites for art installations focused on the rice-growing terraces that the locals had created over a period of more than a thousand years by diverting water using *mabu*, or tunnels created by the meandering rivers. They represented life achievements. As I was exploring these rice terraces for art sites, I discovered that one out of every three or four did not have an identifiable owner. Often the landowners had simply moved away to bigger cities. I imagine it started with one landowner who left, and then others, to the point where it became impossible to keep track. The terraces were left uncultivated for years.

At one point, I had an epiphany as I observed the elderly people shoveling snow off of their roofs. Every year in Niigata, there are about four fatal snow-shoveling accidents. This story isn't just about aging. It is, in part, about the results of not having a community, neighbors, someone to help shovel snow, because the next generation has left. This is how a village breaks down. When the farmers give up farming, it affects a region's lifeways and daily duties, and people's livelihoods.

It's not helpful to think only about the problems of elders in general, or problems of agriculture or the future of Japan. Instead, I believe it is imperative that we contemplate the realities of each individual. My position in response to the elders is this: I don't think others should decide what the elders need. It's rather simple. I am motivated by wanting to see their smiles. I empathize and honor them for having been the cornerstone of Japan. They have been quietly and patiently cultivating in this mountainscape without pretensions, harvesting rice and vegetables and supporting one another. They have been neglected in the national drive toward efficiency, and they don't have ways to express their anger at the situation.

I believe that the various municipal and national policies developed under the name of *machizukuri* (community building) are misguided. It is the elders' enjoyment of life that matters most. It has been seventeen years since I began to think about Echigo-Tsumari, and, within that time, I decided that the triennial's purpose needed to be primarily this: to give the elderly the *matsuri* (festival) experience once every three years in a community that no longer has enough people to have its own traditional annual *matsuri*. It is this central premise that the Echigo-Tsumari Art Triennale is based on.

Why Art?

I believe that art is about discovery, learning, exchange, and collaboration. Art has the power to create experiences and phenomenological effects in ways that may not be readily expressed through photographic documentation. This is why an artwork needs a visitor, and why art in public spaces has such potential power. Since the inception of the triennial, we have sought to produce an art festival with immediacy, one that engages these qualities of art.

This power was proven in Ilya Kabakov's *Rice Fields* in 2000, at the first triennial (see pages 44–45). Since its unveiling, Kabakov's creative process has been experienced in other works as well. The people of the region express support by bringing tea and rice balls to visitors, and in various other ways. As a result, the artwork is not the work of the artist alone but shared by many people. It is a true collaboration. When children visit the rice paddies, the scene comes alive. It is also enlivening when local residents explain an artist's process to visitors. Art is meant to be experienced in the site where it is located and in the surrounding context. This exchange is what moves people, speaks to people, and engages people.

Rejection of Contemporary Art

As we began to realize the triennial, we were faced by a number of problems. We hosted informative presentations for neighborhood residents, community settlements, associations for the promotion of localities, school officials, hospitality businesses, agricultural cooperatives, the media, and local assemblymen, and their responses were extremely skeptical: "There's no way that you can do community building with art!" or "There's no sense in spending money on something as unintelligible and inscrutable as contemporary art."

They were unfamiliar with and resistant to the idea of culture-based community building and creative city planning; they didn't know that there were successful precedents in Newcastle, England, and Nantes, France. There was also widespread opposition to contemporary art, particularly from the regional traditionalist art organizations. It did not help that I was viewed as an outsider; this in itself became a point of contention.

In addition, there was quite a bit of disagreement among the municipalities. There were even communication problems within the municipal offices, for instance, between the person in charge, the manager, the deputy mayor, and the mayor. All of this led to a year's delay of the planned 1999 inauguration of the triennial. The budget was finally finalized in 2000, and it was approved by the large municipal assembly and the executive committee on June 15 of that year. At that point we were scheduled to open the first triennial in one month. This was their way of saying, "Let's see if you can pull this off."

The entire time that we were waiting to receive word about the budget and financing, we were working with the resolve that we would finance the project ourselves if necessary. We continued to work calmly after the June 15 approval, even knowing we would not receive funding for the work that we had done prior to that date. We were in a situation of *hinokuruma*, which has the double meaning of "wagon on fire" and "short of cash." The birth of the Echigo-Tsumari Art Triennale was indeed a very difficult one.

Developing Support

The trends in regional revitalization at the time were "I-turn/U-turn" (promoting a turn toward the countryside among urban dwellers) and ecology (a Japanese interpretive ideology, as opposed to ecological science). One of the key words being tossed around was *machizukuri*, which powerful corporations called upon as an initiative to build new facilities. The idea of *machizukuri* based on contemporary art was unheard of, and therefore rejected by many.

But I believed community building could be explored through public art projects, and I spent three years focused on giving more than two thousand presentations and meetings in order to convince others and gain support for the idea of the triennial. I don't know when I finally experienced some kind of breakthrough. At one point, a manager at the Niigata Prefecture offices unexpectedly said, "We might be able to do something for you," during a meeting. Finally I had persuaded someone to take me seriously, and that feeling was amazing. I had been passionate enough to be willing to fund the triennial myself if I needed to, and I think they understood that intensity. To start finding supporters was extremely encouraging.

Around the same time, a few of the communities finally began to accept us by saying, "You can use this place for artworks." The Hachi Community was the first, cautiously offering the use of *minka* (Japanese traditional homes), roads, parks, and open spaces there.

What I learned from this time is that each of the parties involved—the residents of the communities, the municipal officials, myself—had different perspectives about what *machizukuri* meant. The effects of the collapse of the so-called Bubble economy persisted throughout Japan. While there was strong opposition against building facilities without justification, many were in favor of continuing to build infrastructure despite the economic collapse; the benefits of investing in human capital, however, were not widely understood.

Faret Tachikawa: The Starting Point

"Public art" = "art of the city" was a popular attitude in the 1990s not only in Japan, but also abroad. In this climate, I had directed the urban development project Faret

Tachikawa in Tachikawa City, Tokyo, which in some ways was a precursor of the Echigo-Tsumari Art Triennale.

Faret Tachikawa was implemented by the Housing and Urban Development Corporation as a commercial and business district occupying approximately fifteen acres of a former U.S. military base. Tachikawa City at that point was missing a recognizable local characteristic, a distinct identity, and sought a new long-term plan to develop a theme entitled "The Art and Culture of Kindness," which was to become a feature of Tachikawa through public art and beautification. There was a call for proposals, and our team was selected.

A major emphasis of my plan, which I felt strongly about, was that the art should serve some function for the people living in the place. The art should be integrated into the fabric of the city, as opposed to having some sort of autonomous assertion of its own separate existence. It was also important to emphasize a pluralistic and global perspective on art that would not privilege Western perspectives. I am inspired by the writer Michiko Ishimure, who advocates for art in the margin, what she calls *kishu*, literally meaning "noble birth." I believe that people "on the margin" create interesting and stimulating art. All of these perspectives would carry over into the Echigo-Tsumari Art Triennale.

I do not regard myself as an expert in art history; in fact, my knowledge of Western art history stops at Andy Warhol and Joseph Beuys. But maybe that is OK. I associate Warhol with "mass media" and "consumption," and Beuys with a countercultural response to those tendencies, and I continue to think about those issues and the broadened context of art today. Simply put, I just want to see myriad artworks without focusing on past hierarchies.

Exploring Contemporaneity and Art

In the 1970s in Japan, art was perceived as autonomous. People visited exhibitions and purchased the catalogs to be "cultured," but they lacked a strong sense of engagement, since institutional critique and serious dialogue about contemporaneity were nonexistent.

At the outset of my career there were two ways in which I attempted to more actively engage the Japanese in art. The first was to sell prints. Because they exist in multiples and are relatively inexpensive, this allows for a larger number of people to purchase works, and thereby engage with the artist critically and aesthetically. They ask themselves, "Is this an expensive piece?" or "Is this artist still popular?"

or "Do I love this work enough to have it in my house?" These analyses leave a more lasting impression. My second approach was to focus on making art available to the public instead of shutting it up in museums and galleries. This developed into an involvement with public art.

In Faret Tachikawa, I wanted to address the relationship between art and the people through public works. Public art is often formally well executed but a little mundane. I wanted to counter these tendencies by selecting artworks that had a sense of immediacy and could be phenomenologically and physiologically experienced. I was prepared to accept any criticism about my choices. I began by informing myself about contemporary art by seeing it around the world (as my knowledge of art history ended with Warhol and Beuys). In Germany, I went to see the Münster Sculpture Project and Documenta in Kassel, both of which had a profound impact on how I considered art and museums.

Another influential figure for me is the Spanish architect Antoni Gaudí, who was deeply involved with regionalism and cooperated with craftsmen and carpenters. He represents the quintessential regional craftsman and object maker, and he inspired me to produce a large-scale Gaudí exhibition that traveled to thirteen cities throughout Japan in 1978–79. Gaudí and the Buddhist artists Jyoucho and Unkei have shaped my sensibilities about object making and space.

Then I met Christo, the artist who envelops huge buildings and other spaces. I met him for the first time in Japan in 1990 when he was working on *The Umbrellas*. Christo is significant for me because his work is, in a sense, a counter-voice to Warhol, and he is critically aware of producing his own approach to art. Christo's work has a sense of *matsuri*, or festivity, whereas Beuys's and Warhol's works do not have this quality.

Reflections on Social Movements in Japan

In Japan, a discussion of how to work behind the scenes not only for art installations but also for *matsuri* is connected to an examination of Zenkyoto (the All-Campus Joint Struggle League, active in 1968–69) and Japanese left-wing movements. I found myself involved in the student movements upon moving to Tokyo in 1965, and based on those formative experiences, I have often considered why the Japanese social movements ended in failure.

One problem was their method of organization. For me, the lynching of twelve of their comrades by the United Red Army (Rengo Sekigun) was an unforgettable incident. In the name of "testing" notions of "organization," "justice," and "just cause," twelve people were executed. At the heart of this incident was the intolerant exclusiveness of the organization, which sought to preserve a singular identity by denying diversity.

I work in teams, and I always attempt to create a team of as varied and diverse members as possible. I try to never accuse those who have to quit my team of weakness, but to sympathize with the pain they feel. Out of my reflection on the United Red Army incident came the supportive organization called the Kohebi ("little snake") Volunteers, which has a model of no policy, no leaders, and a fluid definition of membership.

Another point of reference is the rural agricultural movement. The Japanese leftists attempted a revolution in agricultural communities, and instances of corruption and fraud by the local authorities led to its demise. Perhaps this fight for the rural community failed because the movements were generated by values of the urban leftists, as opposed to the communities they were fighting for, and thus they were never able to gain the latter's sympathies. These communities are made up of flesh-and-blood human beings whose individual concerns are not abstract ideals, but the realities of their daily lives. The initial opposition to the Echigo-Tsumari Art Triennale had to do with the fact that the rural people thought they disliked contemporary art, but somewhere in that argument may have been a sort of intuitive reaction against being told by people of "authority" what "justice" is.

Criticism of Japanese Art History

A symbiosis can exist between artists and the general public. A criticism of Japanese art that has existed since the Meiji era (1868–1912) is that it has been overly focused on what can be taught, what can be exhibited, and what can be organized. As I mentioned, Japanese modern and contemporary art had become separate from people's daily lives, partly because of the disproportionate influence of imported trends. It is a pity, for instance, that the Mingei movement (Japanese folk art movement of the late 1920s and 1930s) of Yanagi Sōetsu emphasized the "beauty of utility" in the crafts of everyday life, but did not question the larger structures in which this was embedded.

In part because of my involvement in Faret Tachikawa, and creating there a public art forum that was not only about appeasing "art fans" but also about fostering critical perspectives and considering the local people, I was contacted by Tokamachi City to be involved in its revitalization project. Suddenly, I was inundated with a whole series of social problems that seemingly had nothing to do with art: depopulation, an aging community, abandoned rice fields, a lack of successors, loss of industries. In some ways, however, these were issues that had always been connected to my perception of art.

When I first was going around trying to convince everyone about the triennial, I told them it would be held once every three years, but I only half believed that it could even happen a second time. I heard myself saying things like, "Let's just see what happens with this first edition." As I was meeting more and more people and lecturing and presenting our vision over and over, I asked Wataru Fujiwara, husband of the sculptor Yoshiko Fujiwara, for advice. He said, "It is difficult to convince people with your words by yourself. What if you took advantage of the power of young people to help relay your message?" This astonished me. I had been so immersed in my struggle, I hadn't realized the limitations of my being just one body. I took his suggestion and further recognized the fact that we needed the momentum of something beyond. I resolved to utilize young people on the front lines of our efforts.

This was how the Kohebi Volunteers began. The first experiences of the volunteers were hopeless, as they were shooed away from front porches, sometimes even mistaken for religious or cult proselytizers. Some volunteers were yelled at and went home crying. In the midst of the worst struggles, we abandon heroism.

We gradually learned that the rationale of *machizukuri* meant nothing to the people we were trying to convince. The comments were along the lines of, "Contemporary art? No way!" and "You should be ashamed of supporting such a thing." The Kohebi Volunteers served to gauge the response of people, who lashed out with their raw emotions as opposed to reacting with reason.

But little by little, the volunteers changed the views of the elderly rural farmers. The farmers were conservative and nationalist, and dismissive of the volunteers, labeling them as "strange young people who supposedly do art in the city." The young people were taken aback at first, but then began to explore strategies for how to build understanding. The lesson was to become self-aware of their position in the relationship in order to develop empathy. This has become a major aspect of the Kohebi Volunteers that continues to be upheld. This cross-pollination of individuals of differing generations, backgrounds, and contexts is now a strong foundation for the Echigo-Tsumari Art Triennale.

It takes time and effort to train new and young people to work efficiently and effectively, but I have always felt that inefficiency can sometimes actually create something valuable.

Involvement of International Artists

There are more than two hundred different communities in Echigo-Tsumari, and I aspired to see them directly connected to other countries by inviting international artists to participate in the triennial. I don't mean to place emphasis on the boundaries or divisions between countries but rather on the realities of the nature of a place. This world is perhaps a collection of small localities rather than larger groups based on country or ethnicity. Even the Japanese term *gaikoku,* which means "foreign," connotes curiosity regarding the "outside," beyond the seas, where things are different from this archipelago in terms of lifestyle, customs, and personality.

I once watched a little girl in the park hide behind her mother when she saw a foreigner. She perceived this person as a gigantic *aka-oni,* or "red ogre." The foreigner smiled, but the girl was still afraid, yet curious, peeking out from behind her mother. Finally, she shyly came forth and gave the foreigner a gift made out of paper. We've all witnessed a scene like that. It widens our view of the world when we respond with curiosity to someone unfamiliar.

Let's think for a moment about what globalization has meant for this place on the Japanese archipelago: Imagine the first *Homo sapiens*, the descendants of Eve, if you will, to arrive here from Africa, where *Homo sapiens* first existed about sixty thousand years ago. A global food crisis encouraged mass migration, which in turn resulted in an accumulation of wisdom, as it required communication, tools, and curiosity. This was the first form of globalization. The *Homo sapiens* who came from the south to Japan thirty thousand years ago caught fish and shellfish, built shacks, planted seeds, and cultivated plants. They were in a fertile land. The current population of 130 million people continues to benefit from this richness.

The second period of globalization was marked by the age of discovery and geography. Securing land became a goal, with missionaries, traders, and armies leading the way. Japan was exposed to these influences, but because of geopolitics it was shut out from the rest of the world until 150 years ago, which resulted in the preservation of many aspects of early lifestyles and cultures. The effects of colonialism still exist in the form of so-called modernization.

After Japan experienced defeat and occupation post World War II, it served as a bulwark in the cold war and became a liberal democracy, and an important strategic asset and ally for the American military. Since then we have witnessed increasing emphasis on internationalization and communications, and the liberalization of financial capitalism. Capital became apparent as an ungovernable power; capitalism began to destroy people who lived in harmony with nature. What Japan lost over the course of this process is epitomized in the Echigo-Tsumari region: the traditions of the snow country and its farmlands. Finally, today humans are beginning to recognize their effects on land and climate patterns. We are defined by social structures and physiology, but our foundation is land and climate.

The world of art has been globalized as well. Artworks are sold in an international market and kept in storehouses, just like other types of commodities and precious metals. Their value does not rest solely on the merit of the work, but can be swayed by the media and popular opinion. Nevertheless, artists cannot help asking themselves very simply whether what they create is a manifestation of the human. They inevitably trace how and where their physical experiences have worked toward an understanding of the history of a region. Artists enter the social structure to understand the mechanism of consciousness, look to scientific inquiry to understand the physical universe, and attempt to articulate our place in the cosmos. Art plays a significant role in education and culture. It is the manifestation and creation of humans, and can offer a fundamental image of a society.

When artists from abroad arrive at this place, at first they may not consciously realize it, but the problems they see are not just those of Japan. They exist equally in numerous other countries. Many of the international artists I invite to take part in the triennial are actively engaged with how art can address social issues. The participating artists exemplify the model of face-to-face connections worldwide. I see potential in people who are inspired by artistic and cultural endeavors, lacking the invasive motivations of missionaries, multinational corporations, and the military, especially in this era of finance, information technology, and globalization. This is why I encourage the involvement of international artists as much as possible. These artists have the potential to contribute to a broader context of discovery—discovery by the locals of the international, and discovery by the outsiders of this place.

The decline of regionalism is, I believe, caused in part by a loss of spirit in Japan, as the country had an easy time gaining wealth and geopolitical influence in the decades after World War II. There are, of course, heartwarming stories about people who return home after living in the big cities to start a handmade soba business or a farming inn. But these individual stories do not create large-scale change. It is necessary to change the circumstances and bring in new elements. It is important to involve and accept others. Art is a medium that can move and transform people.

The Echigo-Tsumari Region

Natural Topography, Climate, and Vegetation

Echigo-Tsumari is located on the archipelago facing the Sea of Japan on the Fossa Magna, or Median Tectonic Line, which passes through Honshu (the main island of Japan), dividing it into east and west. The Sea of Japan is connected to Japan's longest river, the Shinano, and Echigo-Tsumari is approximately sixty miles upstream from its estuary at Niigata. The two municipalities that comprise the region, which is at the southern tip of Niigata Prefecture, are Tokamachi City and Tsunan Town. The total area of both Tokamachi and Tsunan is about 300 square miles (Tokyo, by comparison, occupies approximately 240 square miles).

A large part of Niigata Prefecture, including Echigo-Tsumari, was submerged in the sea until some three million years ago. Intense geological activities and tectonic shifts occurred two million years ago. This began the formation one million years ago of the distinct landscapes of dramatic river terraces that form nine steps down the riverbanks in the east, and complex fault surfaces in the hillside terrain to the west.

The climate of the region facing the Sea of Japan is characterized by heavy snowfall in the winter; in fact, it is one of the world's heaviest-snowfall sites, averaging from 100 inches annually to 150 inches in the communities at higher altitudes. This is due to destabilization caused by cold fronts from Siberia combined with heat and moisture from the Tsushima warm front from the Sea of Japan, which yields heavy precipitation (snow) in the watershed of the backbone range of Honshu.

Beech, oak, and maple are the dominant species of trees that make up the deciduous forest plant community. This kind of plant life is common in the region facing the Sea of Japan.

Human History

The oldest signs of human life in Echigo-Tsumari are ruins from the Paleolithic period dating back twenty thousand years, found in the basins of the Kiyotsu and Nakatsu Rivers, which are tributaries of the Shinano River. This was during the Ice Age, when the deciduous bioregion was not yet formed. Humans probably migrated from the landmass of Eurasia along with large animals such as mammoths, *Elephas naumanni* (an extinct elephant of southern Japan), and reindeer.

The Jomon culture, a hunter-gatherer culture that reached a considerable degree of cultural complexity, began when the Tsushima warm front flowed in from the Sea of Japan about ten thousand years ago, producing a climate and vegetation similar to the present. Some of the nation's most valuable ancient Jomon ruins have been found in Echigo-Tsumari. The deciduous forests along the river terraces were places of sustenance for the hunter-gatherer communities, and the winter snow may have even aided in the hunt for rabbits and the preservation of food. The examples of Jomon pottery that were excavated in Sasayama are national treasures and are characteristic of the richness of the Jomon culture in Echigo-Tsumari.

The Yayoi culture first arrived around 300 BCE from the Korean peninsula and brought with it techniques for rice cultivation, but its influence on Echigo-Tsumari was relatively weak, as the Yayoi mainly spread over the plains near the coast. It is believed that Etsu-no-Kuni, the ancient civilization of the region we know as Echigo and Niigata today, was distinct in its relationship to the Izumo farther along the Sea of Japan, and engaged in independent exchanges with the Korean peninsula and Asia.

Echigo-Tsumari landscape

Later, Yamato forces of the Kinki region advanced northward, and Echigo Province was brought under the control of the Yamato sovereignty between the fifth and seventh centuries.

Tsumari-sho, Hataki-sho, and Matsuyama-ho are current place names that align with historical documents dating back to the end of the Heian period (794–1185). Echigo-Tsumari underwent various shifts in power in the time period that followed and throughout the mid-Kamakura period (1185–1333), taking shape by establishing the foundations of the communities that exist today. Some were formed by people who fled during the tumultuous Sengoku (warring states) period (1467–1567), Nanbokucho (northern and southern courts) period (1334–92), and the defeat of the Heike (1185). They came to this mountainous, isolated region and founded agricultural settlements.

By the end of the sixteenth century, local society had stabilized, and developments in civil engineering and land use were progressing. The people developed ways to cultivate a landscape that would not otherwise be suitable for rice farming by creating terraced fields, modifying the curve in the bend of a river to create arable land, and digging holes to create *mabu* (tunnels) to irrigate fields. This labor-intensive work took place over generations.

The production of traditional Echigo linen (*chijimi*) developed during the Edo period (1603–1867), and Tokamachi prospered from sales of the cloth. Descended from the twined cloth (*angin*) of the Jomon period, this traditional fabric was an important part of the livelihood of the farmers, who worked in this industry during the winter months. The fabric was said to gain its unique texture from being placed in the sun on melting snow in early spring. In subsequent decades there was a transition away from hemp to sericulture, or silk farming, and then to cotton production at the turn of the nineteenth century. The region continued to develop as a silk production center during the Taishō and Shōwa periods in the early twentieth century.

Modernization and Ura-Japan

Pressures from Western powers resulted in the collapse of the shogunate system in 1868, which also brought to an end the *sakoku* (closing off of foreign relations) and transformed Japan into a nation-state following the Western model. The transition to an industrial, capitalist economy and the building up of military strength required a new division of labor between the center and the countryside.

The population of the nation during the Meiji period (1868–1912) in 1872 was 32,110,825. Nearly twice the population of Tokyo (779,361) lived in the Niigata region (1,456,831). This points to the very high food productivity that this region possessed at the time. The rural areas sent resources to the center to fuel industries and capital and economic growth. This created a disparity in wealth between these central regions, which became increasingly wealthy, and the rural areas facing the Japan Sea, which led to the term "*ura*-Japan" (back side of Japan) to describe the latter, including the region of Echigo-Tsumari.

The Miyanaka Dam in the Tokamachi district exemplifies the relationship between the central and the rural regions at this time, in that it used the natural resource of the Shinano River to assist in the growth of the Tokyo metropolitan area. The JR East company owns the land and the human-made reservoir by Senju (Kawanishi area) and Ojiya. The hydropower electricity generated here is sent to the Tokyo area and used, in part, to power the JR Yamanote and Chuo railway lines.

After World War II

After Japan's defeat in World War II in 1945, the country was deterred in its colonial ambitions and forced to reenvision its national strategies. Economically, it focused on information and technology-intensive industries and on domestic general-interest consumers, as opposed to exporting industrial products to the colonial markets. Rural resources helped support the nation's postwar recovery. The population of Echigo-Tsumari peaked in 1955, reaching 122,761 people.

Starting in the 1960s, however, people began moving to the cities, a trend that has continued ever since. The textile industry, which had been so important in the region and aided the postwar economy through exports, began losing momentum in the 1970s. Similarly, the agriculture industry began to experience decreasing production policies and regulations. The Japanese government decided to focus instead on industrial products, including automobiles. Agricultural production was largely abandoned and food was imported from abroad. Faced with the dark future of farming, young people fled to the cities in search of work. The agricultural region of Echigo-Tsumari began to be labeled as the "semimountainous region" (a term with marginal connotations), and it continued to experience economic and political decline, aging, and depopulation. Today Echigo-Tsumari has a population of about seventy thousand.

Municipal Mergers

Back in 1888, the Meiji government had enacted a system that officially organized sixteen thousand municipalities; communities had previously been organized informally and traditionally. At the time, Echigo-Tsumari was made up of twenty-five villages, which were reduced in a merger during the Showa era (around 1955) to just six municipalities: Tokamachi City, Tsunan Town, Kawanishi Town, Nakasato Village, Matsudai Town, and Matsunoyama Town.

Later, as part of a ten-year plan called the Heisei mergers that began in the 1990s, the government announced its goal of reducing the country's more than 3,000 municipalities to just 1,000 within a decade, to make the municipal system more effective. Financial incentives and special bonds and tax breaks were offered to encourage localities to participate. (In the end, the number of them was reduced to 1,719 by 2013.) Niigata Prefecture participated by dividing its 112 municipalities into 14 large administrative districts, each of which was based on a central city, and started a regional revitalization campaign, the Risou Plans.

The six municipalities of Echigo-Tsumari comprised one of the administrative districts within Niigata Prefecture, and the so-called Echigo-Tsumari Art Necklace Project was adopted as one of the Risou Plans. As part of the Art Necklace Project the six municipalities jointly worked together to organize the 2000 and 2003 Echigo-Tsumari Art Triennali and developed other major projects, such as the KINARE museum, the Matsudai Snow-Land Agrarian Culture Center NOHBUTAI, and the Echigo-Matsunoyama Museum of Natural Science, Kyororo.

In 2005, all of the six municipalities but Tsunan Town merged, leaving Tokamachi City and Tsunan Town as the region's only two municipalities.

How to Get There

Begin the tour of the Echigo-Tsumari Art Field at the Echigo-Tsumari Satoyama Museum of Contemporary Art, KINARE (telephone +81 25 761 7767) in Tokamachi City. During the triennial you can purchase a passport for access to all art sites there or at the triennial's larger art installations. During off season, tickets can be bought at each site (admission to open-air works is free of charge). Visit www.echigo-tsumari.jp in order to check which works are open to the public.

Driving from Tokyo, the trip of 144 miles to Tokamachi City takes a little over three hours. By train from Tokyo the trip takes less than two hours. Board the JR Joetsu Shinkansen at Tokyo Station or JR Ueno Station. Trains to JR Echigo-Yuzawa Station leave about every thirty minutes. Once you arrive at JR Echigo-Yuzawa Station, change to the Hokuhoku Line and take the train to Tokamachi Station or Matsudai Station.

From Niigata City, take the JR Joetsu Shinkansen at JR Niigata Station. The ride JR Echigo-Yuzawa Station takes fifty minutes. Switch to the Hokuhoku Line to reach the Tokamachi Station thirty-five minutes later.

From Osaka's Shin Osaka Station, take the JR Hokuriku main line "Thunderbird" train to JR Kanazawa Station (a ride of two hours and forty-five minutes) and switch to the JR Hokuriku Shinkansen line. Change at Joetsumyoko Station (about sixty minutes later) for the Echigo Tokimeki Line and switch trains again, about fifteen minutes later, at the Naoetsu Station, boarding the Hokuhoku Line to Tokamachi Station. As an alternative you can also take the JR Tokaido Shinkansen from Shin-Osaka Station to JR Tokyo Station and follow the directions from Tokyo above.

Once you've arrived at Tokamachi, you can arrange for escorted tours or rent a car and explore on your own. Cars can be rented at Toyota in Tokamachi or Echigo-Yuzawa.

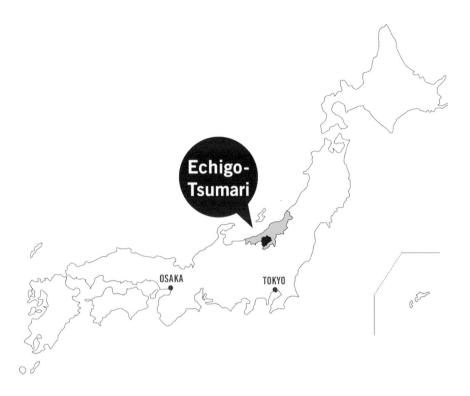

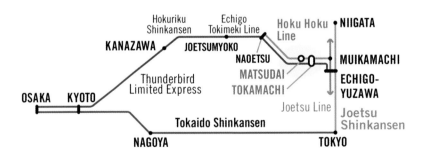

Top: The Ecchigo-Tsumari region in Niigata Prefecture, Japan

Bottom: Public transportation lines to Tokamachi City

001

002

001 Chris Matthews (UK), *Nakasato Scarecrow Garden*,
2000–ongoing
—

002 Richard Wilson (UK), *Set North for Japan (74° 33' 2")*,
2000–ongoing

A Journey: Guided by Art through the *Satoyama* Landscape

Urban design is often dictated by the need for efficiency, which can lead to homogenization within concentrated centers of development. This is reflected in the typical museum experience, in which the artworks are installed close together. In some ways, the rural experience of the Echigo-Tsumari Art Triennale directly counters this need to acquire the most recent information and technology in the most efficient manner. The visitor's experience here is guided by the artworks, which serve as signposts as one roams the landscape. The viewer interacts with the works, and more broadly with the region, while traveling from one work to the next, making possible various levels of intertextuality. The dispersion of the artworks creates fresh views.

This striking landscape and its temporality and seasonality serve as a backdrop for myriad artworks that seek to open the senses to communicate the layers of our ancient genetic memories. A journey through the Echigo-Tsumari region during the triennial is not only a reflection of the localities, but also the tracing and perhaps reinvention of history and time.

Travel! Traveling will teach you many things. Since ancient times the Japanese have studiously practiced traveling as a discipline. The neighboring closeness between indigenous peoples and the Yamato people (the dominant ethnic group in Japan), between the mountains and the plains and the oceans, and between the countryside and the city has turned travel into exchanges between different worlds. But the efficiency of today's travel allows little room for individual effort and creativity. Travel on the shinkansen or on an airplane is simply a means to cover distance and has little to do with the traditional discipline of travel. In Echigo-Tsumari one's arrival at the train station is only the beginning of travel, however, as the vast landscape affords many opportunities to experience the triennial. The journey is enriched by the hard work it may require to uncover and experience the diversity of the many worlds within it.

Kawanishi Area

Matsudai Area

Nakago Green Park
(House of Light)

Matsudai Snow-Land Agrarian
Culture Center NOHBUTAI

Tokamachi Station

Matsudai Station

Echigo-Tsumari Satoyama
Museum of Contemporary Art,
KINARE

Echigo-Matsunoyama
Museum of Natural Science
KYORORO

Tokamachi Area

Matsunoyama Area

Mountain Park Tsunan
(Dragon Museum of
Contemporary Art)

Tsunan Station

4

0 1 2km

Tsunan Area

Nakasato Area

003 Yayoi Kusama (Japan), *Tsumari in Bloom*, 2003–ongoing

—

004 Ritsuko Taho (Japan), *Green Villa*, 2003–ongoing

—

005 Jaume Plensa (Spain), *House of Birds*, 2000–ongoing

006 Shintaro Tanaka (Japan), *The ○△□ Tower and the Red Dragonfly*, 2000–ongoing
Christian Lapie (France), *Fort 61*, 2000–ongoing
Akiko Iwai and Yoko Oba (Japan), *Sound Park*, 2009–ongoing
—

007 John Körmeling (the Netherlands), *Step in Plan*, 2003–ongoing
Text design: Katsumi Asaba (Japan)
—

008 Toyomi Hoshina (Japan), *BUNAGAIKE Botanical Garden "Mother's Tree Midair Garden,"* 2003–ongoing
—

009 Seung Taek Lee (South Korea), *The Tail of Dragon*, 2012–ongoing
—

010 Josep Maria Martin (Spain), *Milutown Bus Stop*, 2000–ongoing
—

011 Yoshiko Fujiwara (Japan), *Homage to Rachel Carson: Four Little Stories*, 2000–ongoing

012 Thomas Eller (Germany), *The human re-entering nature*, 2000–ongoing
—

013 Hironobu Shiozawa (Japan), *Wings / a Trainer of Imagine Flying*, 2003–ongoing
—

014 Tetsuo Sekine (Japan), *Boys with Wonderful Red Loin Cloths*, 2006–ongoing
—

015 José de Guimarães (Portugal), *Signs for Echigo-Tsumari*, 2000–ongoing
—

016 Olu Oguibe (Nigeria), *The Longest River*, 2000–ongoing
Temporary library design: Kazuhiro Kojima (Japan)
—

017 Takeshi Yamamoto (Japan), *Amamizukoshi Tower*, 2009–ongoing

人影は見えないほどに、高く成長した稲穂。

九月。鎌をふるい、一粒も残さず収穫を取り込む時だ。

田から、重い束をやっとのことで運び去る。

十月までにはすっかり乾燥させ、脱穀するためだ。

四月、輝く太陽。
雪は消え、湿っぽい霞が空中を充たす。
ずんぐりした馬が、重い耕作用の鋤を懸命に引っ張る。
春のうちに、田んぼの準備を入念に。
新たな播種と種の植え付けのために。

初めて人間が照りつけ始める。
耕された田の面が、暁の光に光る。
若い芽を……暖まった大地に種を播いてゆく。
……種が、大地から濃く生い立っていくように。

五月の太陽の下に木々は芽吹き、田の水はぬるんでくる。
大地から生えた茎は伸びてゆく。
植え付けられた植物が大地を着飾らせるように。
奇妙な木製の枠、タウクを転がして。

Creating Artwork on Someone Else's Land

There are no conventional gallery spaces or art museums in Echigo-Tsumari. When an artist takes on a project, permission to carry it out must be obtained from the landowner and/or the staff, and the artist must cooperate with the local residents. Initially, many of the residents strongly opposed the idea of inviting artists from outside the region to come and alter sites that they had inherited from their ancestors. But the artists are encouraged to develop projects that engage the sites, deeply consider them, and establish positive relationships with the local residents by building trust in their creative visions. The nurturing of artists' ideas in these communities grew out of a mutual willingness to see beyond the private and individual, which necessitates the stripping of hierarchies to maintain a sharp focus on fostering and communicating ideas among varied individuals.

The Russian artist Ilya Kabakov arrived in Echigo-Tsumari, at my invitation, in the spring of 1999. I trusted his vision and had resolved to support him logistically in any way possible. As we inspected sites, he could not seem to find a suitable location for a project. When we finally decided to quit for the day, we found ourselves at the station for the Hokuhoku train line. Kabakov suddenly stopped moving and stared at the draw enveloping the Shibumigawa River and the sprawling rice fields visible from the station. Long ago, he had envisioned a particular sculptural concept—something like a three-dimensional picture book—and stored it away in his mind. It came back and rapidly took shape when he saw the terraced rice fields. Kabakov said at that moment that he was inspired, and we were taken with his idea.

There are narrative and sculptural elements to the process of rice production: the tilling, seeding, planting, mowing, harvesting, and, finally, sales in a nearby town. Kabakov conceived of sculptural elements that would be planar, profiled cutouts of farmers working in the rice terraces. These elements, when viewed from the vantage point of the train station observation deck, would overlap to relate a narrative.

Through this work, Kabokov expressed a deep and profound respect for the overwhelming labor of the farmers, who exhaust themselves working in the snow country, enduring the challenges and inefficiencies that come with this dramatic landscape. He understood the hardship that was required for the rice production this region is now known for and that the population of the farming community is declining. He sensed the urgency for people to visit this site and understand the complexities of the region.

The landowner, Tomoki Fukushima, had recently suffered a broken femur and had resolved to retire. But even though he knew the land would no longer be used for rice farming, he was reluctant to collaborate with the artist, because the land was sacred to him, symbolizing his ancestors' perseverance and endurance of adversity. Fukushima initially rejected Kabokov's plans but was finally won over by the respect that the artist had for both his particular history and the plight of the farming community. Thus, a connection between Russian and Japanese farming communities was established through mutual respect and empathy.

Despite his physical decline, Fukushima ultimately continued farming this field until the third edition of the triennial, when he retired and devoted himself to caring for his wife. Today we have been entrusted with this terraced land and care for it along with Mr Fukushima's nephew. We call this taking over of abandoned rice terraces the Tanada Rice Terrace Ownership System. When we established the Matsudai Snow-Land Agrarian Culture Center in 2003, we wanted the architecture to incorporate an observation deck for viewing these rice fields. This surrounding area became the Field Museum, and Kabakov's work has become a symbol of agricultural history and culture and the future of agriculture in Japan. It continues to have an impact on viewers and is representative of the Echigo-Tsumari Arts Triennale.

—

018 Ilya and Emilia Kabakov (Russia),
    The Rice Field, 2000–ongoing

The owner of the rice field hosting the Kabakovs' work.

Everything Starts from *Satoyama*

The community, landscape, and culture of Echigo-Tsumari have developed through farming for the past fifteen hundred years. *Satoyama*, the border zone landscape of cultivated, arable land between the forested mountains, is Japan's unique and traditional contribution to the concept of sustainability, based upon interconnections between people and ecology in a seasonal landscape that is exemplified in Echigo-Tsumari. At a time when the paradigms of modernity have yielded problems that can no longer be ignored, *satoyama* may serve as a concept that allows us to reexamine global environmental approaches. Visitors respond to the experience at Echigo-Tsumari as they are enveloped in the distinctive *satoyama* environment. Thus, the dialogue of how people relate to nature is expanded.

019 Antje Gummels (Germany/Japan),
  Traveling Inside, 2009
  The site for this work is a sacred beech forest, protected by community members, that has provided a rich bounty for life since the Jomon era. The path up to the Yakushido Pavilion opens up to a forest of sweeping beech trees deep in the Aizawa community. The eyes fixed on the tree trunks represent the viewer's inner eyes.

020 Hossein Valamanesh (Iran/Australia),
  A Memory of Snow, 2000
  There is a ladder with rungs wrapped in white cotton cloth, creating an illusion of snow in the beech forest. Even during the summer, the snow memories persist via these ladders, which the locals use for dislodging snow from their rooftops in the wintertime.

Art as a Way to Measure the Relationship between Nature, Human Culture, and Society

In 1966, the artist Yukihisa Isobe traveled abroad, away from the Japanese art scene, to study environmental planning and design. He began making work that was ecological in the late 1990s. The research that he was doing as part of fieldwork studies was interesting in terms of its scale and scope. His activities mirrored my thinking about art as a way to capture the relationship between humans, nature, and culture. His position was not to have someone create an "artwork," but rather to see his field research in environmental design and planning as part of festivals. This is where his long-term commitment to the triennial began.

Isobe's projects here have all focused on the Shinano River. Historically, the communities that lived along the banks in the river basin were adjacent and connected. But the Meiji Restoration changed the rivers by damming them and constructing concrete seawalls, and thus divided and isolated communities that lived along the banks of the Shinano, negatively impacting water levels and the river ecology in significant ways. This was followed by problems with water intake caused by the JR East Japan Shinano River power plant.

The history of this relationship between people and the river inspired Isobe to create the *River Trilogy Project*. The piece *Where Has the River Gone?* from the inaugural edition was particularly memorable. The goal was to re-create, using story poles, the path of the Shinano River as it had been one hundred years ago.

But obtaining permission from each of twenty-eight landowners in the Kaino community along the river was necessary for the task to even begin. Their initial response was to object. They were incredulous about the idea of staking poles on farmland. However, upon repeated explanations about the project, little by little, they were convinced. One individual who was against it at first even suggested, "The wind here is pretty strong, and it might be fun to make the change of the wind visible." During the festival, there were seven hundred poles with yellow flags planted along more than two miles of the old Shinano River's snaking path.

Inspired by traces of flood residue from fifteen thousand years ago, discovered on a natural levee at the excavation site in the former Nakasato Village in 1999, and various signs of erosion, the artist and his team demonstrated the drop of the river terrace, by constructing a scaffold, 100 feet high and 360 feet wide. The top of the scaffold showed the highest water level, with each line below marking a five-hundred-year interval.

For the third edition Isobe created the *Farming Music Corridor*, which involved tailoring the rice field terrain made by the *se-gae* method (a method of straightening a curved river in order to increase the farmland) into an amphitheater. This performance stage allowed for distinctive acoustics for the World Taiko Drum Festival, which took place here in 2006 as part of the triennial.

Isobe will unveil the Dragon's Mouth (*Tatsunokuchi*) Erosion Control / Landslide Prevention Dam Project during the sixth triennial in 2015. This region, where landslides have been frequent since ancient times, is referred to as Dragon's Mouth, a metaphor for the dragon's mouth spewing out water. The Dragon's Mouth hillside collapsed during the Northern Nagano earthquake on March

12, 2011, but there were no casualties; since ancient times, the people had been aware of the land's instability and avoided living there. Roads were built later, winding around the site. To prevent further disaster, the Erosion Control Dam is created using state-of-the-art cell structures filled with material from the debris flow; thus, it is made of soil and not concrete. While the service life of concrete is one hundred years, soil is permanent, as it hardens and strengthens day by day. On the opposite face of the mountain is a hydroelectric power plant made eighty years ago. The people of this region thus live between natural disaster and civil engineering, which exemplifies the human relationship with nature in this place.

—

Yukihisa Isobe (Japan), *River Trilogy Project*
021 *Where Has the River Gone?*, 2000
022 *The Shinano River once flowed 25 meters above where it presently flows*, 2003

Terraced Rice Fields as Art

The Shinano River is the longest in Japan. The people of Echigo-Tsumari have always recognized its significance, as its sediment yields large amounts of rich soil. The Jomon culture, a hunter-gatherer society, depended on the harvest found along the river terrace. When rice farming began, it was a struggle to establish terraced rice fields on the mountainsides, but there are no flatlands in this region.

In 2011, the year of the Northern Nagano Earthquake, the region experienced heavy snowfall. Runoff, exacerbated by heavy rains, devastated the Shinano River watershed as embankments collapsed along six rivers. Yet the people continued to harvest delicious rice, because their techniques for farming and maintaining the soil were excellent. The soil here is primary, and in many ways it shapes life. The making of the terraced rice fields symbolizes how rice farming has formed Japanese culture, and this has inspired many artists. Visitors discover the beauty of the rice terraces through the artists' works.

023 Oscar Oiwa (Brasil/USA),
Scarecrow Project, 2000–ongoing
The red scarecrows are life-size silhouettes of the members of the family that owns these terraced rice fields. The small plates on the chests of the figures show the names and dates of birth of the local models for the sculptures. The baby in the mother's arms is a middle-school student today.

024 Takuro Osaka (Japan), *Lunar Project*, 2000
The locals have always cherished the moon, which appears in the reflective waters of the rice paddies before the seedlings have been planted. For the *Lunar Project*, the artist's team positioned eighteen mirrors to reflect the moonlight for approximately ten minutes. The project was performed ten times during the triennial, including nights of lunar eclipse and full moon.

025 Dadang Christanto (Indonesia/Australia),
Cakra Kul-Kul, 2006–ongoing
Inspired by the terraced rice paddies in Echigo-Tsumari, the artist re-creates scenes from his native Indonesia and Bali. Bamboo windmills (*Cakra Kul-Kul*) are placed in the rice fields around harvest season to celebrate the gods. The sound of the bamboo and the smells of the fields envelop the viewer. This work is celebratory and respectful, offering a prayer for an abundant harvest and spiritually connecting the farming communities of Bali and Echigo-Tsumari.

The Significance of Clay in Japanese Culture

Japan is a country of clay. The Japanese understand and utilize clay effectively, as the many uses of clay show, such as bisque-fired Haniwa-Buddhist imagery on clay, the clay and earthen walls of Hōryū-ji, traditional houses with earthen floors, and paths around rice paddies. These last serve as both a boundary and a ridge along the bank. The clay that is used in art and the clay found in the rice fields is one and the same, but the vacuum of the white-walled gallery exhibition space routinely fails to include clay. Culture exists and is born at a site, in connection to a particular location and its plants, animals, and terrain.

In the Chūetsu Earthquake of 2004, the modern rice paddy fields that were in development collapsed, but the long-standing organic rice fields that were made based on underground water and mole routes survived. Niigata is interesting to me, because land use here is creative. It is a snowy, isolated location that requires innovative living. The broader Japanese society can learn from this example as we consider how we can live creatively today. Clay is communicative and can serve as the foundation.

—

The Soil Museum: Mole Pavilion (2012)
Curator: Motoki Sakai
This was an exhibition where visitors could feel and experience earth and soil. Those who work with clay daily include ceramic artists, adobe clay wall craftspeople, soil researchers, and photographers and other artists. Their works exploring clay were featured in the former Higashishimogumi Elementary School.

—

026 Takuto Hiki and Takumi Honda (Japan),
The Clay Path of the Mole, 2012
A solid wall one hundred feet long was formed entirely out of clay from the Gejo district, pounded into place. It is crumbling in spots, because the method does not utilize any sort of medium to reinforce the structure. It thus becomes a metaphor for the land of this region.

—

027 Yoshitaka Nanjo (Japan),
The Pilgrimage of Soil, 2012
Yoshitaka Nanjo explores religiosity through images painted using soil and clay from the sites depicted, for example, the former Higashishimogumi Elementary School, the rice terraces of Keichi, the view overlooking Hakkaisan, and the Shinmei Shrine.

028 Soil Monolith,
Survey of 10,000 years of Japanese Clay, 2012
A 0.4-inch layer of clay takes one hundred years to form; a three-foot layer of clay requires ten thousand years. The sand and rock particles slowly transform with the cycles of plant and animal life. Specimens of strata were collected by painting an adhesive onto cloth, sticking the fabric directly onto geological formations, then peeling it off and displaying it. The result was a representation of time spanning several thousand years. There were browns, blacks, reds, and more colors. The strata were from the Echigo-Tsumari region and other representative locations in Japan.

029 Koichi Kurita (Japan),
Soil Library Project (Echigo), 2006
The earth that we walk on has distinctive colors. Seven hundred fifty soil samplings from Niigata were exhibited at this prehistoric site to share the beauty of the material and to reflect on the history of the land. The vast array of colors covered an impressive area of the traditional domestic space. Niigata is a place rich in water, which broke the rocky ground into different kinds of soil.

HUMAN BEINGS ARE PART OF NATURE / 63

Every Place Reflects the World

Each of the more than two hundred communities in Echigo-Tsumari functions as a unit but cooperates with the others. In a place that was isolated by snow for six months out of every year before motor vehicles, each of the units has developed a strong sense of community as well as of individuality. The identity of the inhabitants lies in this notion of community. Although the Echigo-Tsumari Art Triennale was born out of the Heisei Governmental Merger Policy, the people sought to rediscover their uniqueness rooted in the community units. The local should be connected to the universal world; if you are anchored in a place, it is a universal world.

One cannot live without being part of one's community unit. The community is the center and totality of the world, which is irreplaceable. The artists seek to express the ephemerality of joy, the meaning of existence, and the uniqueness of memories of people living in the snow country.

—

030 Kenji Shimotori (Japan), *Records of Memory, The People of Ashidaki*, 2006–12
Kenji Shimotori wanted to capture what it might be like to be part of the community settlement unit at Ashidaki. After talking with the residents, he created life-size silhouettes of most of them, trying to capture their postures and details, and positioned them in a way that was firmly grounded in the site. The residents recognized who was who. The figures, created for the third triennial, have been reinstalled (by local popular demand) at different sites at every edition since.

031 Jean-Michel Alberola (France), *Little Utopian House*, 2003–ongoing
Jean-Michel Alberola's first work for the triennial was a play on the term "utopia." He proposed a small museum based on the theme "perspectives of the local," by request of the people in the Koyamaru settlement, which is composed of thirteen members of four households: three sets of elderly couples and a family of Bulgarian musicians. The artist saw the lifestyle of the snow country, where one farms an ancestral land while enjoying the changing seasons, as ideal and utopian. He also constructed a pill-shaped community center (*Little Utopian House*) for the second edition and produced the films *Koyamaru Autumn/Winter* and *Koyamaru Spring/Summer* while spending two years here starting in 2007. The films were shown at triennial 2009, and in Tokyo and other cities in Japan and Europe. They were also broadcast in France.

032

HUMAN BEINGS ARE PART OF NATURE /

036

037

038

032 Maaria Wirkkala (Finland), *Found a Mental Connection 3: Every Place Is the Center of the World,* 2003–ongoing
This work highlights each and every member of the settlement of Yomogihira of the Matsudai area. It references the local celebratory ritual of hanging a sedge hat marked with the name of one's house out front. Wirkkala made sedge hats out of aluminum, painted them gold, and put lightbulbs in them. These satellite-like forms became lamps that were attached to forty-six houses in the settlement. Residents turn them on when it gets dark and switch them off when they go to bed. The warm orange light glows and the settlement floats ethereally; the work also serves to affirm the presence of people living there.

———

033, 034, 035 Tetsuo Onari and Mikiko Takeuchi (Japan), *Kamiebiike Museum of Art,* 2009, 2012
This humorous work has continued since the fourth edition of the triennial. Canonical works by Edvard Munch, Johannes Vermeer, Leonardo da Vinci, Jean-François Millet, and other masters are appropriated, but with local residents replacing the figures. Vermeer's *The Milkmaid* becomes a woman pouring raw sake. Da Vinci's *The Last Supper* is reenacted as a community settlement feast. Paintings by Vincent van Gogh and Claude Monet are overlaid with local scenes and sites—microcosms of life in this region. The first floor, which is used as a community workshop in the winter, becomes a kind of farmers' market where local vegetables and crafts can be purchased. Residents talk and blush about their representations. Onari and Takeuchi's work brings laughter and humor to their lives.

Rikigosan (Riki Kato, Godai Watanabe, and Shinichi Yamazaki) (Japan)
036 *Matsuri: A Place to Go Home to,* 2012
037 *The Place to Go Home to,* 2009
Takakura is a beautiful settlement located in the most remote part of Echigo-Tsumari. To get there one must follow a steep, narrow road. To create this work, a shrine that used to be the community's sanctuary was gilded in silver, and sign paintings of community members' younger days and festivities were installed along the road.

———

038 Michiko Kondo (Japan), *HOME Project,* 2009
The Okura community is nestled in the slopes of a mountain between two conjoined tunnels. There is a house there inhabited by one elderly man and a dog. There have been no other residents in the settlement for more than ten years. The artist worked on eleven abandoned houses to transform the spaces where the light spills through the windows to illuminate the people, the houses, and the settlement.

039

040

The Harshest Realities Can Become Effective Themes

039, 040   Christiaan Bastiaans (the Netherlands), *Real Lear*, 2003

Dutch artist Christiaan Bastiaans produced and staged a performance of *Real Lear* for the second edition. It was the opening event for the semioutdoor stage of the Matsudai Snow-Land Agrarian Culture Center NOHBUTAI and was supported by multiple Dutch foundations. Daido Moriyama documented the performance, and a photo book was created under the direction of Daisuke Nakatsuka. The documentation was exhibited again at the fifth triennial.

Ten local elderly men and women are the performers on the stage. They eat and drink while passages of Shakespeare's *King Lear* are delivered, intermixed with personal monologues by the locals. An uncanny tension is created when the dialogues overlap and intersect. Bastiaans initially intended to focus on the societal concerns of the homeless population of the megacity of Tokyo, but changed his topic to the problems that underlie this region and its aging population. Bastiaans spent three months in Echigo-Tsumari interviewing the elderly. The costumes on stage were created by fashion design students.

> *No, I don't want this anymore.*
> *Should I escape to Tokyo? But when I think about it,*
> *I don't even know how to get there, because I'm such a country bumpkin.*
> *And I don't have a place to escape to.*
> *Husband's coming back in the spring.*
> *Then maybe it will be happier around the house again.*

These were voice recordings of the old men and women: their childhood memories, anxieties about getting married, comments on the labors of farming and the poverty of the land, expressions of affinity toward plants and flowers, and notes on the difficulties of life, layered to form a collective voice. King Lear's words mirror the loneliness of these locals, and one might think, "Ah, this is the real Lear." This innovative kind of metaperformance could only be accomplished by having the ten actors, all born and raised in Echigo-Tsumari and still living there today, be both the focus on stage and the subject matter of the performance.

041 Mierle Laderman Ukeles (USA), *Snow Workers' Ballet*, 2003, 2012

The short story writer Yasunari Kawabata once wrote, "The train came out of the long tunnel—and there was the snow country" when describing this wintry region. And indeed, as soon as one passes through this tunnel on the train, the climate changes dramatically; the land is buried in snow for six months of the year. If this were a region with little snow, it would be possible to harvest crops twice, even three times annually. But here, even to bring in one crop is challenging, and the poverty is palpable. But is the history and future of this land so bleak?

Take, for example, the beautiful custom of *yuzuri-michi*, or "making a way for others in the snow." Equal footing for women, as they labor alongside men, is necessary. As they endure the snow and await spring, they wait for neighbors to visit and spend time in deep thought. It's no wonder that this place produced religious leaders and thinkers such as Shinran, Nichiren, and Ryokan.

The negative aspects of *gosetsu*, or "heavy snow," can be changed to positive by artists who create works that avoid the pedantic and instead offer thoughtful reflections on the uniqueness of the locality. Mierle Laderman Ukeles envisioned the hardworking snow workers as a dance team. Her *Snow Workers' Ballet* was a collaboration and performance by the artist and thirteen snow workers, carried out in 2003 and again in 2012.

The Echigo-Tsumari snow workers live in dormitories between November and April, snowplowing between 2 and 7 AM. This task requires athleticism and teamwork, and they are regarded as heroes whose skills are invaluable to the community. Ukeles wanted to honor them and acknowledge their contributions in the summer, during the festival. The applause following the performance was a much-deserved expression of gratitude. The audience flocked to the performers / snow workers after the performance.

In this instance, the foreign eye of Ukeles perceived the local people's labor and expertise as an expressive way of life and created a celebratory performance. The most difficult realities of a way of life can yield rich veins of culture—deep, harsh, yet joyful relationships among humans, nature, and society.

Featuring the Snow

In the 1950s, Tokamachi adopted the attitude of "rather than antagonize, let's befriend the snow." With this decree, the city began the snow *matsuri,* with a subsection for snow art. A variety of snow sculptures are constructed. The various characteristics of snow, such as its white coloration, its translucence, its ability to reflect light, and even its plasticity all lend themselves to artworks. In 1970, GUN, a group of contemporary artists in Niigata, created a beautiful performance that captured the characteristics of snow in Tokamachi.

The winter arts festivals have taken place since 2008. That year, there was an exhibition initiated by GUN that also included the artists Tsuyoshi Ozawa, Yoshiaki Kaihatsu, and Takahito Kimura, and the Australian artists Jeremy Bakker and Ross Coulter. Kyota Takahashi developed a project utilizing LED lighting. In March 2014, fireworks were seen in the snowy Shinano River and a snow-viewing sake party was held.

042 Kyota Takahashi (Japan),
Gift for Frozen Village, 2011, 2012, 2014, 2015
Participants planted ten thousand LED lights. These lights were called "seeds of light" and they bloomed in the snowscape like a field of luminous flowers.

043 Tetsuo Sekine, Kenji Shimotori,
and Shuji Sato (Japan), *Snow Hat,* 2008
Metal pipes with variously formed objects on top of them were placed in a field of snow, and the snow collected on the objects.

044 Tadashi Maeyama (Japan), *Sight of Snow,* 2013
The artist erected a kind of screen that obstructed or cut through the snowscape to make the viewer aware of the surreal quality of the scene.

045 Junji Okubo, Norio Horikawa, and Kenji Funami (Japan), *Snow Country Romance Sled,* 2008
A large sled used to transport lumber fifty years ago was found at the base of the Amida Pavilion and restored with the help of the locals.

046 Snow Art Niigata Unit (Japan),
Snow Picture <Advent of a Big Snake>, 2010
A land art drawing was made in a snowfield using snowshoes and salt to melt the snow.

047 Norio Horikawa (Japan), *Snow Body Art,* 2008
This work features snow imprints of the body that resemble the snow angels children make.

048 Tsuyoshi Ozawa and Kamaboko Art Center (Japan), *Aerial Kamaboko Art Center,* 2011
Semicircular (*kamaboko*) warehouses are frequently seen in Echigo-Tsumari. A blimp resembling the Kamaboko Art Center created by Tsuyoshi Ozawa was flown in the sky during the winter, when the actual center was buried under snow.

049 Jeremy Bakker and Ross Coulter (Australia),
The Space Between Hands, 2012
Curator: Angela Pye
Artists completely foreign to snow resided in Echigo-Tsumari for one month. They made a snow structure that housed four hundred snow forms created by residents as their "portraits."

Gosetsu and Its Relationship to Rice Production

Tokamachi was once known for silk textile production. There are regional brands, such as Akashi chijimi, but much of the work was subcontracted from major companies, such as Kyoto-Nishijin and Kaga Yuzen. Following the oil crises of the 1970s, the industry shrank to a tenth of what it was before. The sounds of the looms that were so prevalent no longer exist today. Traditionally weaving was quietly performed in households during the winter months when farming was not possible.

Rice is grown each year during the more or less one hundred days of sun. When the Oyashio and the Kuroshio currents collide, the monsoon arrives and this climate is particularly suitable for rice production. The Shinano River provides abundant nutrients, but it periodically floods. The terracing of the mountainside requires many years to establish.

The wisdom to create a *satoyama* landscape that complements or works with the climate has also produced a distinctive culture. Silk textiles, sake production, specialty cuisine, spring wildflowers, *kinoko* mushrooms in autumn, and festivals became industries woven into the cloth of the culture. The triennial artists celebrate these industries and help in the effort to revive them.

050 Kazufusa Komaki and Nocturnal Studio (Japan),
House of Silkworms, 2006–11
The community of Yomogihara was formerly known for sericulture. Since 2006, ten thousand silkworms have been grown as a collaboration between the artist and the locals. The *House of Silkworms* collapsed in the heavy snowfall of 2011, but efforts were made to start anew in 2012.

051 Kiyoshi Takizawa (Japan), *Installation for Tsunan—Tsunagari*, 2009–ongoing
An old weaving factory became the backdrop for exploring the notion of yin and yang. T-shirts collected from locals become lampshades, suggesting life forces in the dead of winter. In summer, light fills the second floor, conveying an air of lightness.

052 Takehiko Sanada (Japan), *Tokamachi Monyou*, 2012
The artist has been exploring the textile arts of the region since 2003 and has sought different ways of collaborating with the textile industry in Tokamachi. For the triennial he created an installation using hemp yarn, symbolic for the town.

056

057

058

059

Art Discovers Local Resources

When an artwork is placed at a site, it becomes a way to frame the landscape, whether it is the former Nakasato community, the Kiyotsu River as seen from Kikyohara, or a scene from the Imokawa River. Art can shed light on an environment or give voice to a unique region. This is the power of site-specific art, and the works of Echigo-Tsumari engage with its layers of history and place.

The locals embody the agricultural wisdom of the rice paddies, the farms, and even the community settlements and the tools they use. The artists are inspired to express their discoveries of these various ordinary, essential aspects of life here. Naturally, their work functions as a device to expose and highlight the power of the sites and landscapes it inhabits.

—

053 Akiko Utsumi (Japan),
For Lots of Lost Windows, 2006-ongoing
This work is a window intended to facilitate a rediscovery of the landscape of Echigo-Tsumari overlooking the Imokawa River, which is a tributary of the Shinano.

—

054 Chiyoko Todaka (Japan),
Yamanaka Zutsumi Spiral Works, 2006
Two hundred objects appeared to float on the surface of a reservoir that supplies water to the rice terraces.

—

055 Yasuyoshi Sugiura (Japan), *Wind Screen,* 2006
Two thousand ceramic blocks were stacked for three hundred feet along the edge of the rice terraces.

—

056 Masaaki Nishi (Japan), *Bed for the Cold,* 2000–2011
A white ring floating in a pond moved slowly to suggest the changing of seasons.

—

057 Stefan Banz (Switzerland),
I Built This Garden for Us, 2003, 2009
Stefan Banz created a flower garden in a corner of the abandoned community of Taruda, which can be seen from the observation deck at the ski resort Mountain Park Tsunan.

—

058 Leandro Erlich (Argentina), *Tsumari House,* 2006
A house constructed to appear as though it were reclining was mirrored and reflected. Viewers could lie on the image to create unexpected poses.

059 Yoshiaki Kaihatsu (Japan), *Kamaboko Face,* 2006
Humorous facial expressions were added to numerous semicircular storage structures throughout the region.

—

060 Joana Vasconcelos (France/Portugal),
Message in a Bottle, 2006
An enormous candleholder composed of hundreds of colorful sake bottles lit up the surface of the water at KINARE, the Echigo-Tsumari Satoyama Museum of Contemporary Art.

—

061 Prospector (Japan), *Contact-Ashiyu Project,* 2006
An *ashiyu* footbath was created from more than one hundred scrap wood fittings from vacant houses at the Yunoshima hot spring inn.

—

062 Ryo Toyofuku (Japan), *Tengasa,* 2006
Old, unusable farming tools were collected, painted gold, and exhibited in a vacant house.

—

063 Masao Okabe (Japan), *Can We See Saburo, the God of Winds?,* 2000
Masao Okabe's frottage rubbings collected in the settlements were exhibited in the schoolyard of the former Higashikawa Elementary School.

Forming Temporality and Time

064 Yoshio Kitayama (Japan), *To the Dead, to the Living*, 2000

The conceptualization of temporality is a new approach to art that has been seen in Echigo-Tsumari. Cities can be homogenous places that rob the world of creativity by overemphasizing monetary value and quantification. Even places that hold personal memories and places with histories are quantified. Even art museums are assessed and evaluated based on their visitorship and revenues.

Works grounded in site specificity and heterogeneity, rather than in the "white cube," can change the world around them. Places exist in space but also in time. Perhaps the notion of time—and, more specifically, memories—is one of the few things that cannot be exchanged for currency. Echigo-Tsumari houses many things that have layers of time. Art is revived as an expression of time here, as artists resonate with the specificity of the site.

When I saw Yoshio Kitayama's *To the Dead, to the Living*, I was moved by an expression that could never be achieved in a white cube. This work was intended for the Nakasato settlement and its elementary school, which had been closed. Nakasato receives even more snow than other places in the area. Kitayama secluded himself in this site for three months to complete the work.

As I stepped into the gymnasium, I could hear the sounds of excited children playing. But in reality, there were no children. Filling up the space instead was a large sculptural installation made of bamboo structures with brightly colored papers affixed in billowing arrangements and hanging miniature chairs with wings attached. The stairway leading up to the second floor was entirely covered with photographs of children spending time at this school. Kitayama's collection of newspaper clippings spanning ten years, and drawings of dolls, were displayed in the three classrooms upstairs. There were relics from graduation ceremonies and answer keys. The elementary school began to blur and sway as though it were alive, and I was captivated by the textual and visual evidence turning into its memories.

Kitayama's original conception of the project did not involve anything other than the sculpture downstairs, but one day when he was taking a break, tired from working, he came across the old school materials. As he handled them, the air of the place began to come alive again. The work spoke to the locals too, and they were pleased and satisfied with the installation.

At first, I was happy that there were even just a few visitors per day. Accessing the roads to get there is challenging, because buses cannot pass through; we had to shuttle visitors from the parking lot in our passenger cars. As the artwork gained recognition, however, more and more visitors began to fill the road, which speaks to the work having impact. Kitayama and I understood at that time that the school would be demolished. I wish that we could have kept the space for future installations.

065 Kazuo Kenmochi (Japan),
    Saieiji Temple Main Hall, Kawanishi, 2000
    Kazuo Kenmochi collected photographs of the past
    from the neighbors in Echigo-Tsumari and photos he took
    himself and combined them in a series of albums, thus
    comparing the present with the past. The temple's main
    hall was decorated with the albums and projections of
    the images. It became a space to revive the people who once
    worshipped there.

The Art of Absence

Christian Boltanski (France)
066 *Linen,* 2000 | 067, 068, 069 *Summer Journey,* 2003, in collaboration with Jean Kalman
070, 071 *The Last Class,* 2006–ongoing, in collaboration with Jean Kalman | 072 *No Man's Land,* 2012

I had long regarded Christian Boltanski's work with respect and admiration. When I asked the artist to participate in the first triennial, he said, "You probably don't have a very big budget. Let's see if we can find a way." The result was *Linen.* Since then, he has been featured in every edition and has contributed much to improving the triennial's quality.

Linen was an installation at the Kiyotsugawa riverbed spanning two and a half acres. Several hundred articles of white clothing were collected from residents and flown, hanging, on lines. In the artist's words, the shimmering clothing, reflecting the light as it fluttered, "signified the trembling souls of the residents who lived here, and those who were displaced."

His project for the second edition was *Summer Journey,* which was a collaboration with Jean Kalman incorporating the countless slippers that were left at the entrance of the former Higashikawa Elementary School, the wildflowers in the science room, the extra children's clothes hung in the classroom, and singing coming from the gymnasium. Since the children themselves had disappeared, only these small scraps and memories were left.

For the third edition, Boltanski wanted to reuse that same school. I suggested that I would like the work to be installed permanently. He and Kalman returned to Echigo-Tsumari during a particularly heavy snowfall. Seeing the school deeply submerged, they observed that it seemed to confine itself as if to shelter away from the cold, like closing off memories of place, dense like the snow outside. The many fans in the gymnasium blow around smells of hay and humidity, and a dim light comes from the lightbulbs. In the science room test tubes and flasks are lined up. The last classroom makes us aware of the presence of the people who were there. Members of the community previewed this work before the opening and delivered a number of items related to the settlement and the school. These were stored in the music room, resting quietly. For the fourth edition, Boltanski recorded his heartbeat within this space, which was submitted to the 2010 Setouchi Art Festival as part of the Heartbeat Archive.

During the fifth triennial, Boltanski unveiled *No Man's Land* in the courtyard as part of the grand opening of the Satoyama Museum of Contemporary Art, KINARE. This work had already traveled to Milan, Paris, and New York, but this was the first time it was to be exhibited outside. Boltanski describes it as a response to the Tōhoku earthquake; he visited the affected area. The sixteen-ton mountain of used clothes is occasionally grabbed by a crane device called the Hand of God, and then released. This work greatly challenged and overwhelmed viewers, and consequently became the best-known piece of that year's edition.

070

071

Using Existing Things to Create New Values

Akiya Vacant House Project
073, 074, 075 Marina Abramović (former Yugoslavia), *Dream House*, 2000–ongoing

The Akiya Vacant House Project is described as exemplifying the Echigo-Tsumari style. As previously mentioned, there are a great number of *akiya*, or unused traditional homes, in the region. Often their roofs are collapsed from the heavy snow, and weeds grow inside, but demolishing them costs several hundred thousand yen. The situation is heartbreaking and also a nuisance for the residents of these communities. The triennial seeks to revitalize these *akiya* and their histories through artworks as part of a larger reinvention of the region. More than one hundred such projects have been realized.

One of the pioneers of this kind of project is Marina Abramović, who created the *Dream House*. When the artist arrived in Echigo-Tsumari, she toured many *akiya* in a snowstorm and ultimately selected one with a big roof in the Uwayu settlement in Matsunoyama. An elderly woman in Tokyo owned this *akiya* and used it once a year for the Obon season to pay her respects to her ancestors; it could be rented out the rest of the time. Abramović envisioned a place where travelers could stay and record their dreams. A copper bathtub with herbal bathwater purifies the spirit. Guests wear pajamas specifically designed by the artist, use a pillow made of crystal, and sleep in a coffin-like bed. They are required to record their dreams in a book. The artist's intent was to collect it ten years later and publish its contents. The artist explained her concept to the community members and had them participate prior to the project's public opening.

The Kohebi Volunteers initially assisted in the management of the house, but community members eventually took over. As mostly foreign travelers stay in this house, the locals interact with them and seek ways to improve their stays. The elderly woman in Tokyo now has people to look after the house, and artists, travelers/participants, and locals all play a role in its new life. On March 12, 2011, the Northern Nagano Earthquake damaged the *Dream House* to the extent that reopening would be difficult. But once the decision to restore it was made, the locals fiercely protected the property against the heavy snowfall that winter.

The *Dream Book* was published for the fifth edition of the triennial. Abromović states, "This project was created for the triennial, but something incredible happened. The community members where the *Dream House* was situated decided to adopt the house as their own and continue to care for it. The house has become part of their community. It is the first time for me that my work came out of the art context into real life."

USING EXISTING THINGS TO CREATE NEW VALUES / 107

Top left: Collecting wild vegetables
Top right: *Ubusuna House*
Left: Local women working at the restaurant
Below: The Dolls' Festival at *Ubusuna House*

Revitalizing *Akiya* Connects Humans to Places, People to People

Akiya Vacant House Project, *Ubusuna House* (2006–ongoing)
Producer: Yoshitoki Irisawa, Renovation designer: Kuhihiro Ando
Owner: Fukutake Foundation

Ubusuna House, a thatched-roof house of the Echigo-Chumon style, is one of the five houses of Gannyu settlement. It was badly damaged in the 2004 Chūetsu Earthquake, its foundation so wrecked that the landlord had to move away to Tokamachi City. Master carpenter Fumio Tanaka was consulted to see if the house could be restored. When the undertaking was approved, Yoshitoki Irisawa, editor of *Tojiro* ceramic magazine, became the project leader, and he then recruited a *minka* (traditional house) expert named Kunihiro Ando.

The desire to connect the members of the settlement with visitors led to the idea of a restaurant. I loved the idea of using ceramics as the centerpiece of the restaurant. Irisawa and Ando visited kiln sites throughout Japan to inspect Oribe ware, Shigaraki ware, Bizen ware, Mashiko ware, and Karatsu ware, contacting various ceramicists from these respective villages. Concurrently, Kaori Agi was assigned the task of designing a menu incorporating wild mountain plants and vegetables.

The ceramics are placed in the main room, where a bent tree is striking in its use as a beam. Local foods are served, using only the freshest ingredients that are grown here. In the third edition, *Ubusuna House* received twenty-two thousand visitors and the restaurant earned 12 million yen. Today the restaurant continues to gain in popularity year-round. One of the representatives of the *Ubusuna House* said she has learned a valuable lesson from the visitors, artists, and Kohebi Volunteers all working together. They gave a sense of pride and connection back to the local culture and exemplified values that she had lost touch with. This space represents the aesthetics of the way of life in these settlements.

During the renovation of *Ubusuna House*, the landlord watchfully came by every day on his way to the rice field where he worked. He quietly saw the house he had had to leave behind transformed into a place where people gather. His mixed expression inspired and fueled me to persist in subsequent *akiya* projects.

076 Goro Suzuki (Japan), *Kamado/Stove*,
   2006–ongoing

077 Building facade

078 Takuo Nakamura (Japan), *Surface Wave*,
   2006–ongoing

080

The Hands of People Can Revitalize an *Akiya*

079, 080   Junichi Kurakake and Nihon University College of Art sculpture students (Japan), *Shedding House*, 2006–ongoing

The *Shedding House* is a crystallization of the concept of the *akiya* project. Junichi Kurakake and his students became part of the third triennial following a submitted proposal and drawing. Their ambitious idea was to transform an entire house.

The two-hundred-year-old *minka* (traditional house) at the Hoshitoge settlement is famous for the terraced rice fields nearby. Its landlord had been gone a long time. Kurakake and the students came to Echigo-Tsumari in April 2004 and started by cleaning, from one end of the house to the other. After that, they laboriously deconstructed most of the house, painstakingly carved away at its interior surfaces with a woodcutting tool, then reconstructed it. Midway through, they experienced the Chūetsu Earthquake. They worked at the project for two and a half years, most of them staying more than five months. There were about three thousand participants in total.

A new roof and paper screen doors were installed, and the *Shedding House* was completed. The beams and pillars that were formerly covered with patches of tin were uncovered, revealing a fresh and proud appearance. Today the *Shedding House* has become a travel lodge managed by community members.

The vacant house behind the *Shedding House* was turned into *Croquette House* in 2009. In this one, Nihon University students in art, film, and the performing arts participated. They continue to be committed to community design projects through sport festivals, *bon-odori* dancing, and farming programs.

Students carving the wood floor

081

USING EXISTING THINGS TO CREATE NEW VALUES / 113

Akiya Build New Communities

The wisdom found in the Echigo-Tsumari *minka* is irreplaceable and an important cultural property. The *akiya* project's aim is to preserve the *minka* and find other ways to sustain them in the places where they were built, rather than following the trend of relocating them. The site of a *minka* should be considered for various reasons, including

- to attract individuals and groups from outside to the region of Echigo-Tsumari;
- to revitalize the region by interpreting the *minka,* which symbolizes the local culture and represents the wisdom and environment of the region; and
- to revitalize the depressed local economy by subcontracting to local carpenters and construction companies and giving them an opportunity to learn new skills.

Under these terms, individuals, schools, companies, and organizations have developed the *akiya* as restaurants, galleries, seminar houses, and more.

The Akiya Project Process

1. Gathering of information: Receive information about potential houses from local municipalities.

2. Consultation of Experts: Houses that have not been lived in for some time are often deteriorated and dangerous. Obtain expert structural analysis from professionals and calculate costs for renovation.

3. Contractual Negotiation: Explain the project to the landlords. Most landlords live away from the region. It is sometimes necessary to also receive permission from other family members in addition to the landlord.

4. Artist Visitation: Artists visit the *minka* and propose a project that responds to the region and is specific to the site.

5. Village Briefing: Meet with people in the community and discuss the possible uses for the house and the process. Artists are encouraged to seek help from the community and collaborate whenever possible.

6. Design: Architects determine feasibility of designs and concepts.

7. Cleanup: A century-old *minka* often contains a huge amount of stuff, including old farming tools, utensils, and so on. Keep usable things and dispose of the rest. This requires a lot of labor, and the Kohebi Volunteers play an important role.

8. Renovation, Art Production: The use of local lumber, carpenters, and construction companies is emphasized to revitalize the local industry. Work starts in May when the snow melts. In 2006, dozens of houses were renovated in a short period of three months before the triennial opened.

USING EXISTING THINGS TO CREATE NEW VALUES / 117

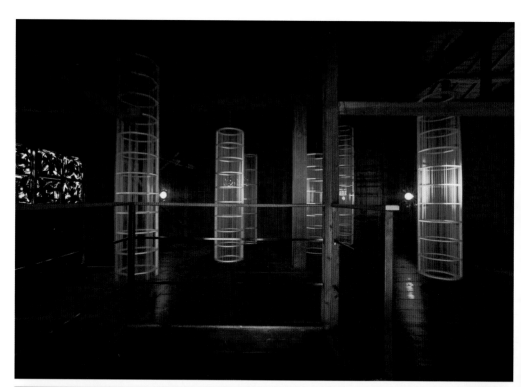

USING EXISTING THINGS TO CREATE NEW VALUES /

USING EXISTING THINGS TO CREATE NEW VALUES / 121

USING EXISTING THINGS TO CREATE NEW VALUES /

081 Takuboku Kuratani (Japan),
Myokayama Photo Gallery, 2006–ongoing
This project opened in the Myokayama settlements
in 2006. Portraits of visitors are taken, with the
understanding that they will be displayed when the
subjects are deceased. Participants range from zero to
ninety years old, and many take family portraits. During
the festivals, university photography students and
graduates run a cafe on the grounds of a nearby former
elementary school.

—

082 BankART and MIKAN (Japan),
Bank Art Tsumari, 2006–ongoing
BankART has organized urban revitalization projects
in Yokohama and opened a new branch in Echigo-
Tsumari. Artists here are involved in architectural
planning, interior design, product design, and textile
design, and host seminars and workshops.

—

083 Bubb and Gravityfree with KEEN (Japan),
DEAI, 2012
This project is located in Tsunan. Sponsored by the
outdoor brand KEEN, sandals from the past and today
are displayed and can be worn by participants.

—

084 Tokyo City University Tezuka
Takaharu Laboratory and Naoyoshi Hikosaka (Japan),
Rei House, 2009–ongoing
The interior of this house is entirely painted in sumi ink.
There are one thousand cooking items, collected into
a sculptural display in the traditional hearth. In 2009, it
was also a functioning Italian restaurant. In 2012, Rirkrit
Tiravanija turned it again into a restaurant, *Curry nō
Curry*, serving Thai curry.

—

085 Harumi Yukutake (Japan), *Restructure*, 2006–ongoing
Covered in thousands of round mirror pieces, the
house both reflects and blends into the surrounding
shimmering and wavering environment. Each of the
mirrors is handcrafted by the artist, and no two are
the same. This was conceived as a temporary work but
became a permanent display.

—

086 Claude Lévêque (France),
Dans le silence ou dans les bruits (In Silence or in Noises),
2009–ongoing
This installation effectively uses the entire house,
each room evoking the life and landscape of Echigo-
Tsumari. In 2012, the artist created *Garden of Semaphore*
by installing twelve-foot steel poles outside the house,
which mirror the surroundings and move with the wind.

087 Tokyo Denki University Yamamoto Space Design Lab
and Kyoritsu Women's University Hori Lab (Japan),
Reflecting House, 2009–ongoing
Myriad stars cover the ceiling. The glass that visitors
walk on reflects a glow from the light. The artists were
exploring the idea of bridging the past with the future
by building a seminar house for university students.
Students from the greater Tokyo area visit, experience
nature, and engage with the community.

—

088 *Tsumari-Tanaka Fumio Library*, 2007–ongoing
Airan Kang (South Korea), *Light of the World,
Light of Intelligence*, 2009–ongoing
Renovation design: Sotaro Yamamoto
In 2007, this former community center was refurbished
into a community library centered on the books
donated by master carpenter Fumio Tanaka, who was
renowned for his work with *minka*. The installation
consists of seven colored, luminous books, which the
artist describes as "books that await and reflect the
viewer's own self." The space is designed to emphasize
the ambiguity between the mundane and the unusual
via contrary elements: artwork books and real books,
the original parts and the new elements of the house.

—

089 Sayaka Ishizuka (Japan), *Ukanome*, 2009
Ukanome is the god of food. The artist attached rice
to 13,800 pieces of string, each about twenty inches
long, which were connected to the ceiling. Items such
as cooking utensils, altar objects, and farm tools also
"float" in this space.

—

090 Haruki Takahashi (Japan),
Landscape Creeper, 2009–ongoing
This house was damaged in the Chūetsu Earthquake.
Ceramic creepers now fill the space. The landscape
patterns painted on their leaves and blossoms are
based on the interview responses of approximately
fifty residents of the Nakasato area, who shared with
the artist descriptions of the places that are most
meaningful to them. The artist then traveled to those
places and painted them onto the ceramic creepers.

—

091 Koji Nakase (Japan), *Gimyo Theater-Kura*, 2003–12
This theater is a renovated *minka* in the Gimyo
settlement that pays respect to the region's history,
climate, culture, and nature. Dances and Japanese
puppet performances were held there to promote
communication and dialogue in and between
communities.

092, 093 Noe Aoki (Japan),
Particles in the Air / Nishitajiri, 2009–ongoing
This was a *ryokan,* or travel lodge, that had not
been used for almost eighty years. The artist has
continued to help farmers plant and harvest rice
since she exhibited her work in the neighborhood
in 2003 and 2006.

———

094 Chiharu Shiota (Japan), *House Memory,* 2009–ongoing
Renovation design: Sohei Imamura
Black wool yarn covers this *akiya,* which formerly
housed silkworms, from the ceiling to the floor. Five
hundred fifty balls of yarn were used, and objects that
locals didn't need but couldn't discard were woven
into the installation.

———

095 Ann Hamilton (USA),
Air for Everyone, 2012–ongoing
Ann Hamilton envisioned this former sheet-metal
workshop as a place for crafting strange tools. The
viewer rings a bell, and the sound connects the house
with the settlement, evoking the craftsmen who used
to work there. Hamilton also has work exhibited in
a mountainous area near the community.

———

096 Antony Gormley (UK),
Another Singularity, 2009–ongoing
Renovation design: Yoshiharu Kanabako
The interior walls of this structure have been removed.
Six hundred eighty-two lengths of cording create lines
spreading between the columns and beams of the house,
seemingly emanating from the center point of a matrix,
evoking the beginning of the universe 13.7 billion years
ago when gravity, space, and time were born.

Schools Are the Community's Lighthouse

Closed Schoolhouse Project
097 Seizo Tashima (Japan), *Hachi and Seizo Tashima Museum of Picture Book Art,* 2009–ongoing
    Renovation designers: Aya Yamagishi, Machika Kubota

Temples have long played an important role in Japanese society. They are places where the people in a region meet and converge, and also where people go to receive counseling or consultations, similar to the function of churches in the West. Since the Meiji Restoration, schools have served this role, and settlements were established around them. The children's development is celebrated at graduations as well as parent-teacher conferences and classroom visits. Sports festivals, always scheduled after harvest time, are some of the more exciting and significant festivals for both the students and the community. Schools are watched over by the people of the settlement, and, reciprocally, the schools watch over the people. In this way, the school is like a lighthouse illuminating the night sea. So long as there is a light burning there, the region continues to assert its existence. With the dramatic depopulation of the Echigo-Tsumari region, the closing of schools was to be expected, but for the residents, and especially the elderly, the phenomenon signals a significant loss of "the guiding light." The communities have a strong desire for the schools to remain, and the triennial has worked to address this issue.

The first artwork utilizing a school campus was Yoshio Kitayama's *To the Dead, to the Living.* Christian Boltanski's *Summer Journey* and Katsuhiko Hibino's *The Day After Tomorrow Newspaper Cultural Department* were featured in the second edition, leading to others in the third. Utilizing abandoned schools has become firmly established as part of the mission of the arts festival, and it has also been incorporated into larger regional planning development. We recognize that superficial proposals from outsiders cannot possibly respond to the desires of the local community. The sustenance of school projects, the requirements of building codes, and the conditions of the old schools present challenges.

The *Hachi and Seizo Tashima Museum of Picture Book Art,* which was born in the fourth triennial, addresses these issues well. Hachi settlement is located in the mountainous area near the center of Tokamachi City. There is a very strong sense of community and identity here (all the residents share the last name Omi), and they have all been involved in the triennial from the beginning. During the first festival, the French artist Bruno Mathon established himself there for a long time. The locals assisted Takahide Mizuuchi, who had worked as a Kohebi Volunteer, in creating a tree house as a tea hut for the second festival. The Sanada Elementary School, which every member of the settlement attended, was closed in March of 2005, then became a site for the artists Vivian Reiss, Rina Banerjee, Haruo Higuma, and Kosai Hori's Unit 00.

The locals wanted Sanada Elementary to remain in use subsequently, and I immediately thought of my old acquaintance, the artist Seizo Tashima, as someone who could transform it for the fourth triennial. Tashima is a painter who has published numerous best-selling children's books. He moved to the Izu peninsula from Hinode-machi after protesting the construction of an industrial waste disposal site there, which emitted cancer-causing chemicals. Later he began his *Memory of Life Force* project, appropriately associated with tree fruits. I wanted Sanada Elementary to have Tajima's powerful works to occupy the space, and it became a center of children's picture books.

Inhabiting an empty *akiya* or school campus can be challenging for artists, because it is not a sterile, neutral white cube; everywhere it bears evidence of its former occupants. Tashima ventured to begin this project at age sixty-seven, and his first inclination was to drag out decades' worth of junk, from the attic to the storehouse. Eventually, he decided to make work specifically using and engaging with this stuff left over. This is how the *Museum of Picture Book Art* began.

The title of the narrative work contained in the "museum" is *The School Won't Be Empty*. This story is about actual former students Yuuki, Yuka, and Kenta, who go back to Sanada Elementary to tell ghost stories and reminisce, and it brings the school back to life. The sculptures that make up the story are made of painted driftwood from the Izu peninsula and other beaches along the Sea of Japan. At the entrance are a few giant *shishi odoshi*, or kinetic fountains, shaped like grasshoppers, which also power the other kinetic sculptures within the building.

Real former students of Sanada Elementary returned to help construct this work, along with Kohebi Volunteers who stayed in the Hachi settlement. During this time the latter cultivated the fields, and some even had babies. Concerts and performances were held there, making it a small hub of entertainment. Now there is also a Hachi Café, a picture book library, and exhibitions, workshops, and concerts held year-round except during the heavy-snow period. This is no longer a school, but, as the title suggests, the building won't be empty anymore.

USING EXISTING THINGS TO CREATE NEW VALUES /

Schools as Keystones for the Community and the World

098 Katsuhiko Hibino (Japan), *The Day After Tomorrow Newspaper Cultural Department*, 2003–ongoing

Katsuhiko Hibino has had a long relationship with the settlement of Azamihira, and his project blooms there every year. He began with the second edition, where he started a project called *The Day After Tomorrow Newspaper Cultural Department*. This endeavor transformed the closed former Azamihira Elementary School into a community keystone.

Hibino received the Grand Prize in the major Parco Japan Graphic Exhibition in 1982 and has since been widely received, making numerous TV appearances. I was attracted to the cardboard sculptural work for which he is known, but I hesitated to involve him, because I questioned whether his kind of art was suitable for the triennial. Ultimately, I invited him to work with the Azamihira settlement, which has sixty members. Hibino's project involved producing and publishing a newspaper at the closed school building. He published every day during the festival and also produced shows, exhibitions, mini soccer tournaments, and drawing contests, which were featured in the publication.

Additionally, he strung ropes all along the school front from the ground to the roof, and planted morning glory seeds. The morning glories, called *asatte-asagao,* or "day after tomorrow morning glories," became symbols of the newspaper and the Azamihira settlement. This project enjoyed a wide reception, and today seeds from the *asatte-asagao* are planted all over Japan. Hibino says that seeds are like vehicles that connect people to people.

He expands on this idea in a work entitled *A Seed Is a Boat.* The inspiration for the project came from an encounter at one of the initial community meetings when he was in conversation with a local grandmother, who didn't understand his concept and proposal, but remarked that she could help by growing morning glories. This demonstrates the positive effect of heterogeneity, which occurs when intermixing various communities, as opposed to the homogeneity that commonly characterizes the effects of globalism.

Despite how busy he is, Hibino enjoys participating in the community events such as the *bon-odori* dancing and *koshogatsu* New Year. The Azamihira settlement has been revitalized.

Asatte Cup (mini soccer tournament)

099 Kyoto Seika University (Japan),
Karekimata Project, 2009–ongoing
Kyoto Seika University proposed a long-term project
at the Karekimata settlement that involves a dialogue
among professors, students, and alumni about
memory, history, and revitalization. Exhibitions,
performances, and workshops take place during
the triennials and beyond.

—

100 *Fukutake House,* 2006, 2009
Soichiro Fukutake produced *Fukutake House* as
an effort to develop an art market in Echigo-Tsumari
and the broader Niigata region. Seven major galleries
from Japan, and other invited galleries from China
and South Korea, came together to create an art fair
environment within empty classrooms and auditoriums.
He envisioned it as a mobile gallery, and it appeared
also at the 2010 Setouchi Art Festival. Starting in 2013,
it was renamed the Asian Art Platform to establish it
as a network center for the broader Asian regions.

101 Tomoko Mukaiyama (Japan/the Netherlands),
Wasted, 2009
Female gender and life are the themes of this
work. Visitors enter a representational womb maze
constructed out of ten thousand dresses, which
leads to a space filled with dresses, handbags,
and scarves (faintly) stained with the menstrual
blood of the artist and the participants who created
this project. Mukaiyama is also a professional
concert pianist who performs primarily in the
Netherlands, and she developed this project while
traveling around the world. She interacted with the
participants and created a piano score about them,
which was performed after the festival in several
cities around the world. Initially, the members of
the settlement were uneasy about the nature of the
artwork but they embraced it eventually and sold
vegetables and gifts to visitors here.

101

Turning a School into a Dormitory

The closed Sansho Schools on the hill of the Kotani settlement have been remodeled into the Sansho House Matsunoyama Community Center. The spaces that used to be classrooms now house eighty clean beds. The members of the settlements lovingly prepare food here. It is used for seminars and group stays and has become a destination for class field trips for students from various places throughout Japan. Here, at this center for engagement, programs developed by members of the settlement offer *minpaku* accommodation and farming/agricultural programs. They have even reinstated the traditional winter ritual, *tori-oi*, in which children beat wooden clappers and circle around the settlement in the snow.

102 *Sansho House*, 2006–ongoing
Renovation design: Shoji Nakamura
Shown here is the cafeteria.
—
103 Aigars Bikše (Latvia), *Good Things from Latvia for Good People in Faraway Japan*, 2006–ongoing
Aigars Bikše created a collection of tools for the members of the settlement.
—
104 Exterior view of *Sansho House*, 2006–ongoing

105 Takahito Kimura (Japan), *Sun and Footprints*, 2012
This was a photographic project in which the locals and the children of Echigo-Tsumari camp school participated in cyanotype workshops. The ceiling of the gymnasium was covered with photographs of clouds, and the floor was covered with water images.

106 Atelier Bow-Wow (Japan), *Making a Veranda for Everyone*, 2011
A workshop was developed to create a sunbathing platform where families and friends could relax after learning how to make their own platforms. They are transportable and can be carried to any desired location for relaxing.

105 | 106 | Traditional event held during the Lunar New Year

School Grounds as Sites for Rural-Urban Exchange

We have been heavily invested in closed schools since the third triennial. The Setouchi Triennale, which was started in 2010 in conjunction with the Echigo-Tsumari Art Triennale, created a school art project in 2013 that successfully brought back three families to Ogishima, allowing for a dramatic reopening of the primary/secondary school. Schools are regarded as places for regional and urban exchange, and thus significant sites for regional restoration. Three more closed schools will be reborn in the sixth triennial in 2015.

At the former Nunagawa Elementary School, we will create a program in which children of the region, along with adults, including the elderly from the community and visitors from the cities, explore four subject areas—household arts, sports, fine art, and music—together with the guidance of professionals: talented athletes, artists, and performers in Japan who struggle to make a living and realize their potential. Here they are able to farm while teaching, living their creative lives while receiving appreciation.

The former Kamigo Elementary School is used as a residence for performance troupes to train, create, and perform in a theater that will be renovated. In contrast to the usual situation in the city, where performance space is costly and troupe members have little time for practice, as they must work part-time to make a living, this space is intended to provide an environment that fosters focused creative production and expands the possibilities for regional performing arts.

We use the former Kiyotsu Elementary School as a warehouse-museum to meet the needs of urban artists and galleries to collect and exhibit large-scale works. People who visit this site see the art that is housed in this facility as well as various site-specific works of the triennial, all while enjoying the *satoyama* landscape.

Outdoor Arcades as Festive Spaces

The issue of revitalizing traditional shopping streets in urban areas of a rapidly aging, depopulated region, with a significantly decreased consumer population, is extremely challenging. Because many of the store owners have considerable savings and multiple properties in other areas of the city, the majority of them are not interested in revitalizing the traditional arcade shopping streets. The Echigo-Tsumari rebuilding began with a focus on the *satoyama* landscape of the surrounding villages and settlements, a historical landscape lost in the urban areas.

After the first triennial, some art installations were created in urban areas as well, in Tokamachi City. But city development on this level requires a broader scope, a substantial budget, and the cooperation of the residents.

During the first triennial, Daniel Buren used the central shopping street in Tokamachi to exhibit *La Musique, La Dance*, with his typical striped banners, which were vividly patterned and a magnificent sight. The enthusiasm of the residents, however, was not enough to continue the project. Since the Genpei battles in the twelfth century, red and white have been used in celebratory rituals in Japan. I want to picture this city center as a celebratory place and conceptualize a way to develop it by utilizing empty properties, stores, and roads for art installations.

107 Daniel Buren (France), *La Musique, La Dance*, 2000
Three hundred fifty tricolored striped banners (in red, orange, and green) were displayed spanning one thousand feet along the outdoor arcade. The vibrant colors brought energy to the summer festival.

108 Rintaro Hara and Yu Hara (Japan),
Kage Matsuri (Shadow Festival), The Kaleidoscope of Summer Festival, 2012
Shadows of the objects and local people of Echigo-Tsumari were cast and traced with black pigment. The disconnected shadow images danced.

109 Hisako Sugiura, Tomoya Sugiura, and Sugiura Laboratory, Showa Women's University (Japan), *Gift in Gift*, 2006
Seven houses were connected by netting. Three of the houses had been destroyed in the Chūetsu Earthquake, and the lace installation outlined the spaces where those houses used to be, almost suggesting a wintery space.

Essay

Echigo-Tsumari and the Art of the Possible:
The Fram Kitagawa Philosophy in Theory and Practice

Adrian Favell

There are two Japans. One is the futuristic, fast-moving, high-tech cityscape of urban sprawl—the Tokyo conurbation that seems to stretch for hundreds of miles north and south, as well as the nation's other important urban hubs. The other Japan is the quiet, declining, rural hinterland, with its crumbling small cities and towns, aging populations, young people moving away to the city, no children being born, and all the old traditions disappearing. In some ways, this is a familiar tale of modernization seen worldwide. But the social polarization visible in Japan is arguably the most dramatic case anywhere, in terms of sheer spatial inequality across an urban/rural divide. Most of the population of Japan is now urbanized. The rest of Japan is, socially speaking, a rural wasteland.[1]

International perceptions of contemporary Japan center on an almost exclusively urban imaginary. This is the vision of Japan beloved by manga, street fashion, J-pop, and designer fans worldwide: the "neo-Tokyo" fantasy of an endless, futuristic urban sprawl, full of weird and wonderful subcultures. Fascination with this image of Japan (and now China) has always been driven by the allure of a rising alternate Asian modernity. In many respects, though, it is a screen hiding a more complicated reality. Japan is not what it was during the boom "Bubble" years in the late 1980s. Yet despite ailing economic fortunes, political stagnation, and social decline in the years since, the Japanese government has thought it wise to continue to invest massively in branding the nation in terms of the fantasy, as a kind of futurist cartoon of "Cool Japan." This peculiar policy got going in the early 2000s and is still high on the agenda despite the shattering disasters of March 2011.[2] Around the same time, in contemporary art, Japan's two best-known international artists, Takashi Murakami and Yoshitomo Nara, rose to fame with a pop art that transposed the culture of Cool Japan into elite museums worldwide. Murakami's "Superflat" movement—which packaged the art of the Bubble years and the decadent times just after as a conceptual art representing a unique national culture—is often all that is known of recent Japanese art internationally.[3]

For many years, this vision has been difficult to dislodge. The kind of art—indeed, the form of social movement—represented by the manifold projects at Fram Kitagawa's Echigo-Tsumari Art Triennale has at the same time been almost invisible internationally. Without a realistic context about the social and economic conditions of contemporary Japan, as well as knowledge of the festival's relation to the contemporary Japanese art world, Echigo-Tsumari can be hard to understand or fully appreciate. Yet as it has grown, and particularly as its patented organizational form was adopted by the even bigger Setouchi Art Festival in the Japanese Inland Sea, social and community-centered art projects dedicated to the economic revitalization of marginal regions, which address the social divides of young and old or urban and rural brought on by economic transformation, have risen to become an almost dominant focus of Japanese contemporary art domestically. Indeed, in the wake of the March 2011 disasters, art speaking to the dysfunctions and social tragedies of the nation— as opposed to art reflecting fashionable urban youth cultures and high-tech futures— has become almost ubiquitous.

The time is ripe for a full international appreciation of the power and ambition of the artistic movement of which Fram Kitagawa has been the central architect. Not least this is because the same social and spatial polarization effects, stagnating economies, lost generations of youth, and potentially desperate demographic decline are beginning to be features of many other highly advanced industrial regions mired in their own long-term economic crises: for instance, the industrial northeast of the United States, eastern Germany, and parts of southern Europe. Through the small but hugely symbolic effects of social interventions enabled by such festivals, Japan offers examples of how these potentially catastrophic and conflicting scenarios of decline might be managed in a rather more gentle, "civilized" fashion—a kind of utopian vision of art and its social relevance for late modernity.

Metabolist Japan: Culture, Economy, and Politics in Postwar Japan

On a clear night in Tokyo, visitors to the twenty-dollar "City View" on the fifty-second floor of Mori Tower in Roppongi Hills are invited to behold the seemingly infinite nighttime sprawl of a spectacular, futuristic city that seems to incarnate everything imagined to be possible of an alternate Asian modernity. Although the Mori Art Museum's exhibitions are often overshadowed by the sublime view outside, the ascent to the fifty-third-floor museum then offers tourists the chance to cap their experience at Tokyo's premier destination for contemporary art: the local equivalent of the pilgrimage demanded of tourists today when they visit Paris, London, or New York and check off the Pompidou, Tate Modern, and Museum of Modern Art. Around them, the Roppongi Hills site, which was completed in 2001 and heavily influenced by the late Minoru Mori's fascination with Le Corbusier, offers a vision of how a "creative city" redevelopment may work in what was a problematic, poor, and crime-infested neighborhood. A multipurpose "city within a city," it has brought back affluent Tokyoites, as well as legions of national and international visitors, to enjoy its self-contained shopping, entertainment, and residential complexes.[4]

Not far away, in an intense, rather chaotic office that is part of Daikanyama's Hillside Terrace—a landmark 1980s architectural development that Fram Kitagawa joined in 1984—lies the headquarters of his organization, Art Front Gallery. Kitagawa does not criticize the Mori philosophy directly, but Roppongi Hills might be seen to incarnate much of the negative vision of Japanese urbanism that has motivated him to take art away from the city into rural areas, in an effort to "cleanse" what the city has become.[5] For Kitagawa, the twentieth century was an age of cities that led to a dark, if not self-destructive, art and culture. The unhealthy alliance of art, urbanism, and commercial interests has long been dominant in Japan. The country's drive to both cooperate and compete with American and European modernity has, in its failure, left a highly urbanized population disconnected and alienated from its origins. For Kitagawa, the spiritual core of Japanese culture has, in its urban incarnation, been replaced by consumerism. "Art should not just sit atop consumerism," he says; a contemporary art museum as a "shrine" atop a shopping mall and office tower block has become a "Parthenon for the modern world."

Fram Kitagawa and the director of the Mori Art Museum, Fumio Nanjo—who has been since the 1980s one of the most familiar Japanese faces in international art and museum circles—have long parallel histories in the brokering of major public art projects over the years. Indeed, their perceived rivalry is sometimes referred to jokingly as the Japanese art "civil war (*namboku senso*) of the north and the south," featuring the Niigata-born Kitagawa (his name means "northern river") versus Nanjo (or "southern quarter"), from Nagoya in the south. Nanjo's vision of "art in the city," which elaborates on the public art installations around Roppongi Hills after a long track record of curating public art installations in many prestigious urban locations in Tokyo and elsewhere, fits well with the mainstream cultural policy of the "creative city."[6] Japanese cities, like so many others internationally, have bought heavily into the vision promoted by urban policy gurus such as Charles Landry and Richard Florida since the 1990s and embodied by landmark projects such as the Guggenheim in Bilbao or Tate Modern in London. In these projects, investment in high-end cultural facilities is said to lead to economic growth by encouraging the talented and creative to engage back in the city, as well as attracting consumers and tourists with spare time and energy to lavish on the arts.[7]

In Japan, first Yokohama, then Kanazawa, then any number of other Japanese cities have explicitly adopted a "creative city" justification for high-end cultural funding—particularly for the construction of museums and the staging of major cultural events—as a core strategy for attracting tourism, service-industry investment, and new forms of urban consumerism and entrepreneurialism.[8] The Mori Building Company, which also cited the "creative city" in its plans for Roppongi Hills, was distinctive in being a private corporate initiative—indeed, one of the significant channels for international investment that started pouring into Tokyo around 2000 after the crisis-provoked deregulation of Japanese banking and financial industries at the end of the 1990s.[9] The city of Tokyo then allowed Mori to build on an unprecedentedly huge site after his slow and costly acquisition over nearly twenty years of the twelve hectares of housing and commercial lots in working-class Roppongi, which he bought up through both carrot and stick pressure on the former residents so that he could create his signature architectural legacy.[10]

This growth-oriented creative city ethos stands as the antithesis of the social movement Fram Kitagawa has tried to create through the activities of Echigo-Tsumari. Art, he claims, should not be an index of modern development, but a way of measuring what has been lost: the distance between urban life and the nature and traditions urban populations have left behind. Nowadays, the modern world only values how fast we can absorb new information. This is why Kitagawa conceived Echigo-Tsumari as a deliberately difficult, "inefficient" experience, one that would force the visitor to slow down and think, not just consume everything, and appreciate the process of tracking down art in abandoned village schools, remote old houses, up a hill or across a deserted field. It would be contemporary art, not packaged as a slick tourist experience, but found in the severest and most unlikely of places.

Minoru Mori's philosophy focused on cleaning up the city and reeducating urban populations through the sublime experience of art and culture in a futuristic museum. Kitagawa's concern, on the other hand, is that art has replaced a God that has been lost. Art is in danger of becoming a commercial accessory to urban living, as well as a fig leaf for ever more urban development. It is, he says, a strategy that merely reproduces the Western, U.S.-dominated system. It worked well for Japan to be in this subservient position during the "air pocket" of the Cold War years. It gave the country the financial Bubble and delusions of world economic power. But this is when the Japanese lost their ethics. Art was then co-opted in the 1990s and 2000s to keep the development logic going.

The inward investment of global capital that followed into Tokyo through the Mori Building Company and other multinational corporations at the turn of the century was the heralding of a full normalization of Tokyo as an archetypal global city—that is, a megalopolis embedded in global circuits of power and capital, but increasingly disconnected with and distinct from its own national hinterlands.[11] Notably—with the partial exception of Fukuoka and Sapporo, which have different, regionally embedded economies linked with China and Korea—other cities in Japan have only suffered in the shadow of Tokyo's ongoing growth. The postwar era of modernization has been a long story of rural to urban flight, in which declining rural homelands were romanticized as the *furusato* regional origins of populations going to the city.[12]

Yet the hinterlands were also, in the heyday of the Liberal Democratic Party (LDP), quite well sustained through political subsidies (on farming, construction, landscaping, and industrial production), and then later on the promotion of *shinkansen* package tourism to the regions.[13] This is what political scientists refer to cynically as "pork barrel" politics, feeding all the most important interests and constituencies to keep them politically pliant. But after the Bubble of the 1980s, many of Japan's formerly industrially rich regional cities as well as environmentally rich agricultural terrains went into decline and shrinkage. As globalization swept in finally at the end of the 1990s, much of this was impossible to sustain. Meanwhile, the farming hinterlands have declined ever more sharply, with an almost ubiquitous flight of youth to the cities, and the dramatic aging of agricultural populations that will never be replaced. Moreover, from 1995 onward, the birth rate started to decline to one of the lowest in the developed industrial world. By 2005 the population itself had started to shrink, with an unprecedented proportion of very old people as the postwar baby-boomer generation aged. Japan can almost certainly look forward to a population approaching 25 to 30 percent smaller by 2050 (declining from approximately 130 million to 100 million), with anywhere between 30 and 40 percent past retirement age (that is, never again working), and with a current annual loss of about five hundred thousand people a year (in other words, a city the size of Nagasaki).[14]

Tokyo, whose population and wealth has continued to grow, and whose performance almost entirely accounts for the much-trumpeted "growth" spurt of recent Abenomics (named for Prime Minister Shinzō Abe), is thus the exception, not the rule.[15] The international fixation on the global city of Tokyo as Japan of course masks this, but it fits well with the older, utopian visions of an ever-expanding, almost entirely urbanized Japan that were dreamt of by the famous metabolist architects and planners of the 1950s and 1960s.[16] The brilliant students of Kenzō Tange, himself inspired by the planning dreams of Le Corbusier, in fact invented a distinctively futurist culture for an Asian growth machine that was thought internationally to have no culture but one of imitation. As documented by Rem Koolhaas and Hans Ulrich Obrist, this *Project Japan* of the metabolists for a while wedded modernist utopianism to vast bureaucratic governmental ambition, such that Japan invented almost a new stage in "total urbanization," akin to the theories of Henri Lefebvre.[17] What the world saw was the organizational wonder of the 1964 Olympics and the cybernetic playground of the 1970 Osaka Expo, registering these then as the image of a future Asian superpower.[18] When all this developed further into the high-tech consumerist wonderland of 1980s Bubble Japan—in which the Japanese economy began to even overtake and surpass America's—many of these oriental dreams seemed to be coming true. It is not a coincidence that Mori's most enthusiastic and well-funded shows at the Mori Art Museum have been about architecture and made an explicit link via Le Corbusier between metabolism and the idea of Roppongi Hills.[19]

Orchestrating this metabolist economy at the urban core, the LDP nevertheless lived off the support of the conservative heartlands, which they bought off via subsidies and regional backhanders. This was the heyday of the infamous "iron triangle"—the tight relationship between government, bureaucratic planners, and business corporations—which drove the unprecedented growth machine of the postwar boom years.[20] But after the Bubble, with Japan's economic decline, the ongoing urbanization and centralization of wealth and power in Tokyo made the regions politically much less significant. Niigata is a case in point. At the heart of Echigo-Tsumari, the small textile-producing city of Tokamachi and the rice farming areas around it was one of the most archetypal, solid heartlands of conservative LDP power during its long postwar reign. This carefully cultivated constituency was the power base particularly of a local Niigata politician, Kakuei Tanaka, a prime minister in the early 1970s who was long the dominant, charismatic figure in the region. He ensured that the prefecture would always have its huge agricultural subsidies, and he created a flow of lucrative public-works projects for businessmen in the region.

Kitagawa himself comes from Niigata, and this part of the region is very symbolically important for Japan as a noted area of top-quality rice production. Expensively subsidized, with price tariffs on foreign rice as much as seven times above international prices, the prized rice is grown on artificially terraced fields on hillsides. This built schools in villages where children's numbers were declining, paved rivers and hillsides in case of any natural disaster, and laid out roads and tunnels through mountains that led nowhere. Export industries were also imposed on the region in place of the self-sustaining local economy. Tanaka's most famous scheme was to persuade the state to finance the Jōetsu northern *shinkansen*, which runs through mountains and over rivers from Tokyo to Niigata city, stopping in many tiny towns and small tourist resorts en route. It was the notorious *shinkansen* that went nowhere. Huge new railway stations were constructed to attract people and development, but all they did was enable the population of Niigata to move out even more quickly to the city. After the 1980s Bubble, when the money ran out, the region was left with empty schools and public buildings, failed businesses, a disappearing population, and grass growing over brand-new highways. Meanwhile, the last generation of farmers was getting too old to manage its subsidized fields.

This is the desolate landscape into which Kitagawa has brought his ideas. It is a Japan largely forgotten in the overwhelming focus of its "modern" arts and high culture in the central cities. In Japan, modernity was urbanization, and funding going to the regions to sustain culture was superfluous. When Prime Minister Junichiro Koizumi reached the inevitable conclusion and pursued the downsizing administrative reforms of the Heisei mergers in 2005 as a way of reforming the politics of his own party, costs were cut dramatically by ending subsidies and amalgamating infrastructures.[21] Koizumi set out to drastically reduce the number of municipalities in Japan. This led to a massive downgrading of local governance and a real abandonment of many isolated areas. The big political game during the 2000s was to focus on deregulation within urban economies to enable Japan to embrace global capitalism and to lose as little as possible of the international investment that was being seriously sapped by the spectacular rise of other Asian cities.

When disaster struck in March 2011, this was a disaster too for the nation in terms of potential flight of business and investment. Ironically, though, the tsunami has been the best news in a long time for the iron triangle and its growth-obsessed reflex of blinkered modernism: particularly for the old construction industry (think "concrete futures"), as Tohoku has been reconstructed through state-subsidized, cookie-cutter development. The state and its planners ran roughshod over the protests of many architects and urbanists who said it was time for new thinking about the form of these cities, especially their overwhelmingly old and isolated populations, and the wisdom of coastal sprawl. In the end, though, it has been (cheap) new homes for all—as opposed to acclaimed architect Toyo Ito's much-fanfared hopes[22]—as well as new, even higher, concrete sea defenses that still would have failed in March 2011. With undignified haste, Abe has sought to switch back on the nuclear reactors that have powered the overlit neon-bright cities of Japanese consumerism—despite the supposed Japanese aversion to the nuclear—and the energy politics that embed Japan most firmly in the emprise of American domination.[23]

And then Tokyo got lucky once more, when it was chosen, partly on a sympathy vote, partly because of the economic and political collapse of rival bidders, to host the Olympics in 2020. All of a sudden Cool Japan was back up and running. It was a new chance to plan an earthquake- and radiation-threatened international development bonanza that might hark back to the now almost innocent-seeming heyday of Japanese futurist development in the 1960s, especially, of course, 1964. Whatever happens in 2020, it is clear that the Tokyo Olympics can only mean the further concentration of capital, culture, and power in the central city at the expense of the declining regions, and doubtless the further proliferation of fantasies of "neo-Tokyo" at the expense of "real" Japan.

A Back-to-the-Country Alternative?

The Echigo-Tsumari Art Triennale has since 2000 sought to offer a response to this apparently one-way drift of culture, economy, and politics. Something different needed to be done to create a civil society that was missing in Japan's relations between the state, its cities, and its consumer populations.[24] Fram Kitagawa's anti-urban philosophy, now sharply defined by the praxis of the six Echigo-Tsumari Art Triennali (this count includes the one taking place in 2015), is a complicated mix of soft traditionalism and sharp political critique.

Echigo-Tsumari is inextricable from romantic rhetoric about the heartland *satoyama*, which equates the in-between landscape of cultivated arable lands between wild, forested mountains and urbanized "civilization" with the soul of Japan. For Kitagawa, *satoyama* symbolizes the unity of the Japanese with the landscape, as well as a lost sense of rural tradition among the populations who now can only experience an alienated modern urban life. Kitagawa wanted to bring these people back to the countryside, to experience an art festival there that could reconnect them with their regional roots. He frequently states that the quality of this society has to be measured by the smiles of old people cared for by the festival.

At the same time, his philosophy is partly hard-nosed policy orthodoxy: the festival is justified and promoted with the language of rural revitalization, which seeks salvation through new tourist economies, cultural production, and attracting young people and families to move away from cities. In these terms, it suggests an alternate "creative economy" intervention that encourages the rebuilding of social and community relations that have been severed by postindustrial division: *machizukuri* (community building), as it is commonly referred to. Part of this too is a consensual concern with putting culture into employment as a form of bottom-up social welfare, particularly for isolated, aging populations. Yet Echigo-Tsumari can also be read as a radical politics: angry about a Japanese modernism that seems to equate Japanese modernity entirely with the inequities of international global capitalism, and which bluntly challenges the mainstream fixations of exclusively "urban" contemporary commercial art in Japan. As the curator Raiji Kuroda has eloquently pointed out in recent writings, part of Asian modernity necessarily is a struggle for emancipation from this (Westernized) hegemony, such that the unfinished drive of modernity in Asian contexts can indeed be expressed in the local, the vernacular, the traditional, and the peripheral.[25]

Kitagawa, born in 1946, is an archetypal postwar baby boomer who passed through the crucible of 1960s radicalism. Arriving in Tokyo for university in 1965, he was swept up into student politics as an activist and radical, while pursuing a course of study at Geidai (now Tokyo University of the Arts). He studied Buddhist art, which set him on a career of gallery dealing and brokering art for corporations and publications, which brought him into partnership with urban developers. The business activities appear to have been mostly a means to an end: a way to pursue his passion for curating and taking high art to the people. His first major touring show, on Antoni Gaudí (1978–79), was followed in 1988–90 by the landmark antiapartheid art exhibition *Apartheid Non! International Art Festival*, which toured to 194 locations around Japan in a huge articulated truck marked by a red balloon.[26]

Some of Kitagawa's early writings develop novel ideas about the social and community relations involved in curating these shows, breaking with an emphasis on locating Japanese contemporary art in a narrative of high (Western) modern and postmodern art. Kitagawa's art theory ends, he says, with Andy Warhol and Joseph Beuys. Beyond these two figures—who represent, respectively, the ironic embrace of market forces and the antidote of social art by and for everyone—the theory melts away into a different practical understanding of art as a public good embedded in social and political movements. Kitagawa's interest in the vernacular and the traditional makes him a populist, and he is very insistent on how even elite artists coming to Echigo-Tsumari must immerse themselves in the social and political realities of life and work in the region before they begin their residencies. Crucially too he has come to reject the typical elite art reflex in Japan of trying to play the "Western" or "global" game by inserting "Japanness" into a global conceptual or commercial discourse. This was a talent well developed, for example, by On Kawara and, later, Takashi Murakami, to establish themselves internationally.

The struggle of the late 1960s led to a comprehensive disillusionment with left-wing politics, which Kitagawa associates with the internal executions of Rengo Sekigun (United Red Army) members in 1972, at a time when radical politics created a cult-like fanaticism. From this, Kitagawa learned an emphasis on diversity and pluralism in his organizational practices, at least in theory. The second key element, common to others working in the impossible cultural void of the 1980s Bubble, was the necessary cultivation of links with an enlightened segment of corporate Japan, in order for any kind of progressive cultural agenda to develop. His involvement in the development of architect Fumihiko Maki's Hillside Terrace in Daikanyama from the early 1980s on provided a base for Art Front Gallery. It was part of the parallel invention, for the first time, of a genuine commercial contemporary art scene in Japan, with initiatives such as the Seibu Sezon Museum, the rise of galleries such as Fuji TV and Touko, and the opening, with commercial sponsorship, of the influential art space Sagachō.[27]

Kitagawa retained his radicalism, however, in terms of his relation to the mainstream art world. Ever since he was young, he explains, he wanted to destroy the existing art system. This is a familiar refrain among nearly all the pioneers of the Japanese contemporary art world in the postwar era. The crucial aspect to note in many of the contemporary art initiatives of the 1980s was the lack of support— indeed, total lack of interest—from the government. Kitagawa's anti-apartheid commitment, however, reflected the liberal and cosmopolitan mood of 1980s internationalism in Japan, which was predominant in the contemporary art of that period, such as in the work of the Kyoto performance group Dumb Type, and emerging pop art figures such as Shinro Ohtake and Yukinori Yanagi.[28] Indeed, Kitagawa and Art Front Gallery provided the young Yanagi's first representation, an influence that has been visible in his later large-scale, land- and community-based works.[29] A more typical response to the void of the 1980s was the macabre visions of Arata Isozaki's postmodern turn against metabolism: ruining his own Tsukuba development or reruining Hiroshima.[30] Elements of Isozaki's philosophy of the "incubated cities" underlining the ruins latent in all modern development can be read into Kitagawa's subsequent turn away from the city to embrace the quieter ruins of the Japanese countryside. Isozaki's later Artpolis projects in Kumamoto, commissioning community-oriented architecture as a tool of urban regeneration, were also forerunners of Echigo-Tsumari in certain respects, as Lynne Breslin discusses in this volume.[31]

With his track record of touring shows, as well as the public events at Daikanyama, Kitagawa was selected in the early 1990s to direct the huge and well-funded Faret Tachikawa public art project, which, when it opened in 1994, became a defining step in the development of a new mode of curating public works, as well as in the uses of culture to sustain urban development.[32] The remote western suburb of Tokyo had housed an American military base, which returned large areas of open space to the city when it was closed. A new city complex of offices and shops was constructed on part of the site, but it was deemed to need branding in terms of an innovative cultural image. Kitagawa followed his instincts and insisted on commissioning artists to create work in-situ and working with officials and locals to make sure these artists could use the everyday materials of street furniture and city utilities as part of their work. As Kitagawa notes in the art guide to the site: "Artists discovered urban functions such as exterior walls, parking ramp walls, lighting, bollards, and tree grates, and turned them into artworks, as if birds had looked for places to build a nest."[33] Kitagawa's methods and idealism, here, can be contrasted with the more conventional public art initiatives of Fumio Nanjo, a much more mainstream political and corporate operator with a background in finance, who had worked for the Japan Foundation and had already curated some of the most important international shows of Japanese art of that era.[34]

Faret Tachikawa was still relatively conventional in its selection of international artists and the tendency for some works to simply be monumental sculptures in incongruous sites. It signaled, however, new possibilities for the notion of a public art project, in particular the creation of new urban spaces for art.[35] Kitagawa's innovations here reflected and built upon a wider artistic movement in which he was central. Notably, there are many parallels with Shingo Yamano, the current director of Yokohama's remarkable community art project, the Koganecho Bazaar.[36] From a similar postwar generation, Yamano was a formalist artist who had been involved with the radical art school Bigakko in Tokyo.[37] Frustrated by the conservative commercial art scene in 1970s Tokyo, he set up base in Fukuoka, where from the early 1980s on he began to organize new forms of public art, carving out radical art spaces in a conservative and skeptical city.[38] This led to the Museum City Project, in which the young Raiji Kuroda was a cocurator: a series of art events that, from 1990 until 2002, established a paradigm for street-based art and commercial funding (in the absence of much government support) before similar initiatives had been attempted in Tokyo, and approximately contemporaneous with the parallel organizational innovations of the Young British Artists' movement in London.[39]

Kitagawa and Yamano became linked up during the 1980s in connection with the early career of Tadashi Kawamata, the artist from Japan most associated with developing the notion of the "art project" outside conventional museum spaces.[40] Yamano also helped stage Kitagawa's *Apartheid Non!* tour in Fukuoka. Kawamata is renowned internationally today for his outdoor wooden architectural constructions that "grow" on the outsides of public buildings, or that create new public spaces and meeting places out of improvised and often discarded materials, usually with the complicated involvement of local communities and public/private networks.[41] His articulate conceptual reflections on the two possibilities of the art project— of the work being the "live" documentation of work in progress, and the work being the unique product only possible because of the in-situ materials, personnel, and conditions that he happens to find at the site—are hugely influential sources of ideas feeding into the later Echigo-Tsumari projects, in which he has taken a prominent part.[42] In Fukuoka, in 1983, Yamano created for the young Kawamata one of his earliest platforms for an interior installation work (*Otemon, Wada-so*) by negotiating access to an empty apartment in a commercial building that was about to be knocked down in the name of early–Bubble era development. The next year Kitagawa curated Kawamata's controversial *Under Construction* at Daikanyama Hillside Terrace, a large, open building site improvisation around the location, which was forced to close after two weeks because of public outrage at the "mess" (like a building site) it created for local businesses and shops.

These connections lay the foundations for the next generation of art organizers, several of whom are key players in the current contemporary art scene in Japan. A somewhat younger art producer, the present director of BankART in Yokohama, Osamu Ikeda, was also involved in the *Under Construction* project as part of the radical architectural group PH Studio. He later was involved in remodeling the articulated truck used in the *Apartheid Non!* touring exhibition, and he worked as a curator for Kitagawa's Hillside Gallery at Daikanyama. Ikeda has thus worked closely with Kitagawa, Yamano, and Kawamata over the years—he cites Kitagawa and Kawamata, along with the architect Hiroshi Hara, as the three "masters" who taught him—and BankART is today one of the most important city-funded public art centers in Japan.[43] BankART also runs an artist residency site in a remote part of Echigo-Tsumari, and Ikeda is often mentioned as a possible successor to Kitagawa at Echigo-Tsumari or Setouchi.

Ikeda has continued to work with Kawamata over the years, and in *Expand BankART* (2012–13) staged an enormous installation work by Kawamata involving the whole waterside building in Yokohama. While they share much of the same conceptual philosophy about art projects and art in the community, there is a distinction between the radical idealism of the older Kitagawa and Yamano, and the rather more pragmatist Kawamata and Ikeda. Kawamata takes pains to note his political distance from the older pair, who are the last (or youngest) of the baby-boomer student radicals who experienced the end of the 1960s and early 1970s as students.[44] Born in 1953, Kawamata is too young to have engaged with those formative moments very directly (notably 1968 and then the year of ANPO in 1970). To this list of interconnected figures, we can add Tokyo University of the Arts professor Toyomi Hoshina, who was an early partner of Kawamata at Geidai and is the creative force behind many of the Ueno-based public art initiatives of the last couple of decades. And then there is Ikeda's direct counterpart in Tokyo, Masato Nakamura, director of 3331 Arts Chiyoda, who works in Hoshina's oil painting department at Geidai. Since his break with his early partner, Takashi Murakami, Nakamura has gone on to become the most influential public art organizer in the city—first with his insurgent street-art events in the early 1990s (Gimburart and Shinjuku Boys Art), then the neighborhood collaborations of Akihabara TV (1999) and Command N (in Kanda), then the enormous art center project 3331 Arts Chiyoda in an abandoned middle school, and most recently the ongoing TransArt projects utilizing unused corporate buildings in the city.[45] This list would not be complete without mentioning the partnership of Junya Yamaide and Tadashi Serizawa, who run similar programs in Beppu in the south; Yukinori Yanagi and his projects in Seto; and the activities of two frequent associates of Nakamura's 3331 Arts Chiyoda, Katsuhiko Hibino (whom I discuss below) and Hiroshi Fuji (like Yanagi, a Kyushu-born social artist, now director of the Towada Art Center). This constellation of figures can be viewed as a who's who of social and community art pioneers in Japan, all circling around Kitagawa, who together lie behind most of the innovations seen in the country in the organization of this mode of art event.[46]

As a result of the intense exposure he received with Faret Tachikawa, Kitagawa was invited in 1995 by the Niigata municipality of Tokamachi to consider the possibilities of a new kind of revitalization project in this remote, declining region. As he was born in Niigata, the place held certain emotional possibilities but also presented a totally different kind of environment from the urban art projects he had been hitherto involved in, with its run-down towns and declining villages, and the small city facing further infrastructural shrinkage with the Heisei municipal mergers. Kitagawa's practical conversion to the idea of rural art might be dated here, although certainly his interests in regional traditionalism go much further back. Other sources may include one particular feature of post-1960s radical art in Japan: rural theater and performance art communes, such as Tadashi Suzuki's Togamura company in Toyama (from 1976 on), or Min Tanaka's famous *butoh* school (Body Weather Farm) in Yamanashi from the late 1980s on.[47] The latter example also became a site in which artists would be invited to do in-situ work, although it had more the ambience of a remote sect than a rural revitalization project.

An interesting parallel can be drawn between these innovations and the later Echigo-Tsumari, particularly as it has gone on to embrace performance as very central to its mission. Kitagawa, though, has surely gone much further in seeking to win over locals as participants and eventually also co-owners of the art projects sited in their villages. Initially there was zero obvious interest or support among the wider public—which is mostly elderly and very conservative—for the idea of contemporary art as a tool for regional development on their doorsteps. The Heisei mergers, first proposed in 1995, did provide a kind of opportunity, though, in that they enabled the large-scale imagination of a new kind of art festival that, with some central support, might embrace the whole region, with all of its distinct localities and landscapes. The somewhat strangely named "Art Necklace Project"—as Kitagawa called his proposals—can be understood as a way of picturing the ring-like constellation of localities centered on Tokamachi, as well as the small town where Echigo-Tsumari would establish its base, Matsudai, out of which different and distinctive art projects, like jewels, would emerge. And, with poetic resonance, running through the heart of this region was the great northern river itself, the Shinano, which had brought life to the area but had been battered and tamed by public construction works.

In the five hard years it took to get the first edition of Echigo-Tsumari off the ground, Kitagawa faced opposition at every turn from local politicians and the general public. Very few villages were willing to be involved in the initial events planned, and Kitagawa recalls the anguish of many young volunteers who were literally chased away from houses they were visiting as they tried to persuade the locals of their good intentions. As he also recounts, basic funding for the first event was not approved until the last minute. Kitagawa's work as a tireless advocate and persuader, part radical visionary, part suited CEO, needs to be interpreted and evaluated perhaps in the light of the work of his younger peers in art organization, such as Nakamura and Yamaide, or indeed other artists with heavily organizational modes of work, such as Kawamata and Yanagi. In all of these cases, trends in international art theory that now centrally consider the crossover potential of curation-as-art, or art and architecture as convergent forms of organizational and/or spatial practices, would have no trouble recognizing the work of these artistic figures as falling within the current avant-garde of much recent international contemporary art.[48] Nakamura, for example, is still emphatically an artist, even though his artwork consists for the most part in the complex negotiations required to stage his curated public art events: the extraordinary struggles and patient persuasions needed in Japan to get public officials, the police, local association leaders, corporations, business entrepreneurs, residents, and so on all to assent to and sometimes participate in such events.

Yet, excepting Kawamata, none of the artists or curators listed above has ever received this kind of recognition internationally, essentially because of a wider ignorance about Japanese contemporary art since the 1990s. By the same token, Kitagawa's work is worthy of assessment as a form of spectacular logistical art-as-curation, although he himself is very clear in not wishing to claim the status of artist. But certainly he has pioneered organizational possibilities in Japan that others have followed and elaborated as artists. Echigo-Tsumari, with its three hundred square miles, more than two hundred works, more than two hundred locations, and countless volunteers, participants, and (even) unwilling bystanders, can in these terms count as the pioneering epitome of what is becoming Kitagawa's most important Japanese and international art legacy: a case study in what might be called "the art of the possible." A good indicator of this is the large number of social and relational artists involved regularly at Echigo-Tsumari—for example, Tsuyoshi Ozawa, who has provided a series of characteristic works developed out of local amenities—as well as many architects, particularly those whose work has increasingly involved the cultivation of socially embedded "spatial practices," for example, units that respond to public involvement and vernacular forms, such as Atelier Bow-Wow and MIKAN.

The influential Japanese art critic and curator Yusuke Nakahara was one of the first to recognize the paradigm shift in contemporary art heralded by Echigo-Tsumari. In his influential essays for the early triennials' catalogs, along with noting how

TOP: Aerial view of 3331 Arts Chiyoda, converted Rensei Junior High School, near Akihabara. Courtesy of 3331 Arts Chiyoda.
BOTTOM: Asia Photography and Image Center, former Myokayama Primary School, Echigo-Tsumari (2012). Photo by author.

Echigo-Tsumari opens up new possibilities for a largely unexplored idea of nonurban art (and hence—as Kuroda's argument suggests—a potentially nonurban modernity), he stresses already the potentials for a "reconsideration of the formats for what we describe as art exhibitions" as well as the potentials for "change not only among the residents of the region but also among the participating artists themselves."[49] This paradigm change would become even more significant as the emphasis of artworks at the triennials shifted from made-in-situ objects to the reutilization of empty and abandoned houses, schools, and other sites.[50]

Kitagawa's sober assessment in his closing essay in this volume describes some of the difficulties in organizing the early editions, particularly the first. The resistance of villagers to cooperating with the sometimes-intrusive plans, and hard challenges about the money spent on works, opened up the organization to criticism that it was all top-down art parachuted in from the city with little respect or sensitivity to the locality. Critics have also pointed out that the environmentally concerned Echigo-Tsumari received funding from a prefecture, Niigata, that had benefited from the opening of the Kashiwazaki-Kariwa nuclear reactor site. This lies only about thirty miles from parts of the triennial site. Kitagawa denies any connection.

In retrospect, some of the monumental-style works have not worn so well. The permanent open-air installations of early editions were often the typical plastic or steel works so familiar from global art fashions of the 1990s. These toxic monuments sit incongruously in their beautiful surroundings and over the years have cost a fortune to maintain. But criticisms of the inefficiency of the event in terms of travel and logistics miss one of the key defining points of Kitagawa's philosophy: that the art at Echigo-Tsumari can only be consumed slowly, often with difficulty (both physically and practically), and often with many detours and deviations along the route, such as chatting with locals or trying out regional food and resting points. These are the everyday pleasures en route to a new connection with the landscape and its population, even if visitors fail to see all or much of the art. "Slow art" is, he asserts, the antidote to the "sickness" engendered by the fast consumer life of the city.

Already in the first events, as Nakahara has pointed out, there were innovations that have gone on to be signature elements of the triennial as a philosophy and practice. Notably, there are works of land art that take their meaning from their dialogue with the landscape or the locals with whom the work had to be painstakingly negotiated. And, after Kitagawa began to successfully negotiate permission, the opening up of abandoned *akiya* and, in some cases, entire abandoned villages gave a new purpose to the art installations. Artists began to use the houses less simply as alternate "white cubes" and more as sites in which the artwork itself becomes part of a renovation and rehabilitation of a dormant dwelling—or perhaps an entire community. Empty schools, meanwhile, are hugely emblematic, as Kitagawa says, because they are sites that remain central to communities beyond their use as places to educate children, and because there is no more stark emblem of the waste involved in past public works projects: building plans that showered construction businesses with contracts when there was literally no future for these communities because children were not being born in sufficient numbers.

Echigo-Tsumari faced a funding crisis at the end of the 2006 edition, but by then a new key figure, Soichiro Fukutake, had become involved. Fukutake sees himself also as a pioneer of social and community art because of his long investment in the Naoshima art site, which has become internationally famous and is much better documented in English-language literature than Echigo-Tsumari.[51] As with all of the statements made by the now-senior art pioneers about the exact sources and lineage of their ideas, Fukutake's later pronouncements about his own philosophy and engagements benefit from hindsight and a change in the economic mood of the times, something that has enabled observers to recognize them as part of a wider national or even global zeitgeist.[52] As CEO of the huge Benesse corporation, Fukutake (born in 1945) was a multimillionaire and notable art collector. His return at age forty to live in his native region, and the renewed connection this gave him with islands of the Inland Sea, convinced him that he needed to think differently about economy and culture.[53] He felt he should make some kind of investment in the locality. Although a beautiful and legendary part of Japan, the Inland Sea between Kyushu and Kansai has been largely despoiled by industrial development and heavy shipping, with some islands facing a combination of environmental damage and population extinction. His work in Naoshima, the first of the art islands of Setouchi developed by Fukutake, was initially motivated by a fairly straightforward idea of tourism-led revitalization. By the beginning of the 1990s, Fukutake was amassing a serious collection of contemporary art to add to his Claude Monet collection, building a museum on Naoshima to house it. He was particularly inspired by the young Kysuhu artist Yukinori Yanagi, of whom he became a significant patron. The site was later complemented by Tadao Ando's stunning Chichu Museum, as well as the innovative art house projects in the nearby village of Honmura, in which artists and architects have built a quite extraordinary series of permanent installations. Other sites have been added on the island since.

The experience of Naoshima at times has the feel of a rich man's playground, like the secret base of a James Bond villain, with its uniformed attendants and immaculately tendered privatized spaces. But in the art houses, the involvement of site-specific logic and local participants becomes more apparent. In particular, Fukutake's eventual support of Yanagi's vastly ambitious project on Inujima (which dates back to 1994)—to convert the whole despoiled island into a massive art project—engaged Fukutake in an explicitly postindustrial, postgrowth mission in Setouchi. Yanagi envisaged Inujima, with its dying *genkai shūraku* (a village with a population below the limit of sustainability) and its massive abandoned copper factory, as a kind of Gesamtkunstwerk that could reflect on the demise of modernization in Japan.[54] With Fukutake's funding (approved in 2001) and the name Seirensho (Refinery), he would eventually stage a series of installations of Fukutake's memorabilia of the extreme nationalist novelist Yukio Mishima in a spectacular, environmentally sustainable museum designed by the young architect Hiroshi Sambuichi, which opened in 2008.

From this point on, much of Fukutake's activities have been devoted to using art to help restore and protect the Seto Islands and their populations. Here his mission clearly dovetails with Kitagawa's investment into Niigata; once Fukutake discovered Echigo-Tsumari in 2003, he became a staunch supporter and eventually copartner in the event. Inspired by Kitagawa, who was first brought in as acting director of the Chichu Museum, there was an expansion of the ideas for the island projects into a full-blown festival: the Setouchi Art Festival, which had its first iteration in 2010.[55] Using the exact same model as Echigo-Tsumari, and sharing its environmental and rural reinvestment ideals, it took place in a much more tourist-friendly location and became a stunning surprise success. Nearly one million visitors crammed local boats and buses during the sweltering summer and fall months to visit the fabled "art islands."

Kitagawa's central role in Setouchi ensures that both events effectively share the same philosophy. Its originality can be illustrated briefly by two impressive examples of social and community art from the festivals, one from Setouchi, one from Echigo-Tsumari. The well-established Berlin-based artist Chiharu Shiota, who was selected for the Japanese Pavilion at the Venice Biennale in 2015, has been an important participant in both events. At Setouchi, there is her work *Distant Memory* (2010) on Teshima, a beautiful midsize island to the east of Naoshima. Teshima was one of the worst examples of poisonous industrial dumping and population decline, and has

Top: Chiharu Shiota, *Distant Memory*, house and installation on Teshima Island, Setouchi (2010–ongoing). Photo by author.
Bottom: Katsuhiko Hibino and students, *The Day After Tomorrow Newspaper Cultural Department*.
Former Azamihara Primary School, Echigo-Tsumari (2012). Photo by author.

been a central concern of Fukutake after his initial attempts to clean up the damage on Naoshima. Shiota, a widely recognized installation artist who has mostly worked in a museum and art-school context, asked Kitagawa how she could ever work on this remote island. He told her that to build her installation, she should smile a lot and talk to locals, and ask them what to do and how to do it, something that transformed her own practice and some of the reluctant villagers around her.[56] The resultant work is a converted rice house and former social hall, in which Shiota built a time tunnel made out of collected windows from empty houses around the Seto Island sea, and which connects a rice field at the back to a view (out front with the sea behind) of an old house in which the first child in seventy years was born on the island. It is one remote work in the sometimes impossible "slow art" treasure hunt across the islands at Setouchi, as in the rice fields and mountains of Niigata at Echigo-Tsumari.

Some of the bigger-scale projects, meanwhile, such as Katsuhiko Hibino's *The Day After Tomorrow* at Echigo-Tsumari, echo the many other school conversions that have become a feature of both events. In the very remote village of Azamihara, the former school and other buildings have become the long-term residences for young students who make a newspaper daily about the not-so-trivial lives of the old people in the village, articulating Hibino's ideas about spreading the seeds of the future throughout Japan. Part of Kitagawa's philosophy thus taps into the resources of what might be called Japan's "creative surplus":[57] the masses of redundant art and design school wannabe creatives (*kuriieitaa*) who come from the city to join the festival as volunteer *kohebi* (little snakes) and in Setouchi as *koebi* (little shrimps). Many projects explicitly connect this "lost generation" with the other "surplus" population of modern Japan they would never normally meet: the aging villagers in remote locations.

For Kitagawa, the success of Setouchi after the more modest (albeit growing) numbers posted by the Echigo-Tsumari Triennale over the years might be seen as a double-edged success. Setouchi has been quite well visited and documented by the royalty of global art, and now clearly overshadows the festival that really gave it its central ideas and model. Fukutake has been a sponsor since 2006 of Echigo-Tsumari but he has concentrated more of his legacy on the Inland Sea. It is said that his personal fortune is so large that his endowment could finance Setouchi festivals every three years for the next one hundred.[58] The second Setouchi Art Festival in 2013, which still involved Fram Kitagawa's organization in a management role, expanded its ambitions and took place in three installments over one hundred days through the year. Forced to diversify its sponsors since 2006, Echigo-Tsumari has faced a more uncertain future, particulary in 2012 and 2015. And, as so often is the case with large-scale movements in Japan driven by charismatic individuals, Kitagawa's very personal hand in the festival also means it is hard to imagine how it can continue beyond his own intensely personalized involvement.

Post-3.11 Perceptions

Without a doubt, there has been a remarkable change in mood within Japanese contemporary art as a result of the triple March 2011 disasters (earthquake, tsunami, and nuclear reactor meltdown).[59] Partly to do also with the opening up of arts funding to explicitly put culture to use in the postdisaster period, many artists have shifted their agenda to embrace social and community-related practices that, in some respects, fit with the philosophy that Echigo-Tsumari has always embodied. There is certainly a danger that the ensuing rush of research and publications on this topic will start to frame the art coming out of Japan as if it has gone through this sea change only after 2011.

The reality is, of course, that the lineage of Kitagawa and his associates as pioneers goes back to the origins of social and site-specific art projects of the 1980s. For sure too the watershed of the disasters of 1995 was important: the moment at which many NPO-related artistic initiatives got going, largely out of the wider frustration felt in society at the poor governmental responses to the Kobe earthquake. Moreover, the broad social disasters implicit in the trends in social polarization and rapid rural population decline are, in a sense, an even deeper source of artistic concern. Rather than seeing 2011 as a turning point in Japanese art after the vacuity of the Cool Japan era, then, it is better to read the current period as a time finally ripe for an understanding of Echigo-Tsumari as a critical expression of the Japanese postgrowth condition, which effectively dates back to the end of the Bubble, in 1990.

For sure, the international art world was interested in other things during the heyday of Murakami and Nara, and Echigo-Tsumari has not always leveraged very wisely the big-name foreign artists and curators who have been expensively brought in to give the event more international credibility. Other problems dog the idealism of Setouchi and Echigo-Tsumari. One is the obvious tension between social and community goals and the implicit and sometimes explicit gentrification that occurs as visiting tourist populations effectively displace and "repopulate" the disappearing villages and villagers in beautiful remote rural locations.[60] Certainly there have been significant aspects of counterurbanization visible in some parts of Echigo-Tsumari, but this on the whole appears to be a sensitive and engaged younger population, opting to try to make a new life with and among the older residents.[61] Criticisms of heavy-handed management, misunderstandings, and unhappy locals have been reported in some studies about the on-the-ground realities of Echigo-Tsumari.[62] It is also often pointed out that Kitagawa's idealism about his pluralist organization and its inclusive philosophy is belied sometimes by the intense exploitation of the young workers as volunteers and the strict, almost autocratic hierarchy of the organization. Kitagawa certainly expects all of his organization to be as committed and engaged as he is, and orders are dispatched in the conventional Japanese corporate style, from top to bottom. Meanwhile, most of the projects in Echigo-Tsumari need to be judged on a case-by-case basis in terms of their involvement with, and responsiveness to, local populations. The positive examples here cited by Kitagawa could be contrasted with others. In the end, though, it can hardly be surprising to find that public art management in Japan is a largely macho business. Fram Kitagawa is a tough political and financial operator, and the contradictions in his philosophy are probably part of the inevitable price of making the vision work.

Perhaps a more substantive issue is the growing critique among art critics of the "sociological turn" in Japanese contemporary art, for which Kitagawa and Echigo-Tsumari certainly are now the dominant paradigm. These issues evoke classical theoretical concerns about any art that may get subsumed in its social or political function, as opposed to locating its value in autonomous aesthetics and art history.[63] In some recent interventions led by the young art critic Futoshi Hoshino, there has been a concerted attempt to attack the overwhelming dominance of social and political criteria in the exhibitions and debates about art and architecture since 3.11, invoking a series of points made by Claire Bishop, initially against proponents of "relational aesthetics" in contemporary global art, notably Nicolas Bourriaud and Grant Kester.[64] There is always a danger that standards of aesthetic quality and independence get sacrificed in artworks that are seen to be involved in engineering some better community. Moreover, there is a distinct whiff of political co-optation about so many of the social and community art projects embraced as part of community rebuilding since the disasters. What is the warm glowing feeling of *kizuna* (community ties) that they are supposed to evoke but a fake nationalist discourse of unity to cover up sharp social divisions and conflicts produced by the same government and its neglect of marginal populations? And does not the social and community return to roots also sound a lot like a new *sakoku* (a national closure to the outside world as before 1853) descending over Japan as it has withdrawn into a post-3.11 defensiveness?

These criticisms echo fairly explicitly those articulated by Bishop in her writings. Drawing on the writings of the French philosopher Jacques Rancière, she has sought to reassert the need for an independent modernist critique in artwork. Squarely rejecting the "sociological" justification for art's significance, and the illusion of replacing art objects with amorphous social processes that seem like social work, she might well read Kitagawa's work at Echigo-Tsumari (if she were aware of it) as a bad example of the naive "community art" she attacks elsewhere, such as in 1970s Britain, when artists did lots of face painting with kids or provided free meals to pensioners. The danger is that artists end up being a kind of replacement welfare state for "neo-liberal" governmental agencies keen to withdraw their support of the most vulnerable sectors of society. This point has also been made specifically in Japan by some critics of the recent "social turn."[65]

One can certainly question whether many of the elite art-world heroes feted by Bourriaud and further canonized by Kester and anthologies of global social and relational art by other authors really do escape these criticisms. Their almost complete lack of coverage of Japanese artists and art organizers, who, as we have seen, have been widely active in this area since the 1980s, is a glaring omission. But in terms of the actual criteria set up by Kester to pinpoint the originality and power of certain types of socially engaged collaborative art practices, the large-scale and unique ambition of the Echigo-Tsumari art festival does fulfill much of what he emphasizes.[66]

Rejecting the modernist notion of the all-seeing artist who creates art as a form of rupture and critique, Kester argues that such projects prioritize five things: locality and duration; the downplaying of artistic authorship; conciliatory strategies and relationships with specific communities; the process of collaboration as an artistic end in itself; and novel organizational forms similar to NPOs and social movements. Much of what is being done in Echigo-Tsumari and Setouchi clearly fits these criteria.[67] While the art objects seen in rural festivals such as Echigo-Tsumari do vary wildly from the sublime to the kitsch, and from the charmingly vernacular to the incongruously toxic, where projects have become intrinsically engaged and involved local populations integrally, a new kind of social art has emerged. The art effectively lies in the new social relations that are created, not (really) the objects or final products that are ostensibly the cause of these interactions. What I hope to have illustrated is how well these projects tap into the demographic and social drama of postgrowth Japan in decline: the spectacular backdrop of chronically aging populations and masses of redundant, overeducated youth.[68]

To defend Kitagawa against some of the suspicions of the oversociologization of art, then, we need to read Echigo-Tsumari against some of his own positions. Clearly the aesthetic quality of the work matters, and, looking through past catalogs, one can sometimes question whether too many of the domestic artists involved were indeed engaging in the kind of the feel-good art-as-social-work that Bishop criticizes. The weaknesses of some works become less significant, however, when we try to conceive of the "big field" of Echigo-Tsumari as precisely that: a huge regional artwork in itself, in which Kitagawa's organizational and curatorial practice is the central component. That is, thinking of the triennial as akin to how Yukinori Yanagi apparently conceived the Inujima island project: as a Gesamtkunstwerk involving the villagers, the decaying buildings, and the desolate postindustrial or agrarian landscapes. On this scale, Echigo-Tsumari can be viewed globally as a unique, ongoing experiment in relational and community art, in which the art organization itself takes on a significant social welfare role in "postpolitical" spaces of society in which government has largely abdicated responsibility.[69] Here, the oft-quoted policy ideal of rural revitalization and community building—*machizukuri* (literally, "making a town")—may be thought of in a broader, metaphorical sense as the rebuilding of society through the creation of new social relations and public spaces from the distinct populations brought together by the art festival. While much can be said critically in theory about this kind of intervention, the spectacular ambition and achievements of Echigo-Tsumari over the past two decades may also silence such criticism when viewed up close. Fram Kitagawa's guide to the most important works of the triennial and the key concepts of his movement can then stand as a legacy of truly global importance.

Echigo-Tsumari's significance is therefore much more than just a commentary on the fate of Japan. In the near past, Japan's urbanization represented the future. Art and culture were hitched to this growth-driven development, whether in underwriting the building of big new urban monuments or in aiding inner-city renewal. In post-Bubble, postgrowth, postdisaster Japan, that future may be over. Lessons are slowly being learned. But rampant urbanization still rules in many parts of the planet. In America, the dominance of urban life over rural alternatives is absolute. This will go on as long as there are fresh fields and deserts on which to build new housing tracts, and still more oil to put in the tank. In Asia, and China in particular, the frenzy of overdevelopment seems unstoppable.[70] Europe faces many of the same problems that are felt in Japan today. Someday all these places will sober up. When they do, they may look again at Japan's recent experiences for inspiration. Even before the disasters

Top: Aerial view of Inujima Art Project Seirensho (2008). Copper refinery site conversion and museum
by Yukinori Yanagi with architect Hiroshi Sambuichi, Inujima island, Setouchi. Photo by Road Izumiyama.
Courtesy of Yukinori Yanagi and Miyake Fine Art.
Bottom: View from rooftop of Mori Tower in Roppongi Hills at night. Photo by author.

of March 2011, with its post-Bubble gloom and shocking urban-rural divides, Japan faced urgent issues in managing its own decline and the social divisions it heralded. Japan in the 1990s and 2000s may, in other words, be everyone's future tomorrow. It is, for sure, not a happy prospect. The Echigo-Tsumari Art Triennale and its cousin event in Setouchi help visitors think about a different kind of future. It is a future a million miles from the futurist vision Japan gave to the world at the Osaka Expo in 1970. And it is such a long way from the Cool Japan experience given to tourists at Roppongi Hills on a clear night in neo-Tokyo.

Notes

1   This essay extends on the chapter about Fram Kitagawa
    in my book *Before and After Superflat: A Short History of
    Japanese Contemporary Art 1990–2011* (Hong Kong: Blue
    Kingfisher, 2012), 174–84. It reflects a substantial body
    of work conducted in collaboration with the architect and
    urban theorist Julian Worrall of the University of Adelaide
    toward a book we are planning on social and relational
    art and architecture in post-growth Japan since 1990. I
    would like to acknowledge especially the help of Rei Maeda
    and Miwa Worrall of Art Front Gallery in the research for
    this essay, as well as many discussions with Julian, the artist
    James Jack, and the independent curator Eiko Honda.

2   The policy is usually traced to the inspiration of an
    American journalist writing about how Japan might replace
    its reliance on ailing manufacturing and financial sectors by
    turning to its pop culture and high-tech industries. Douglas
    McGray, "Japan's Gross National Cool," *Foreign Policy*
    (May–June 2002): 44–54.

3   This is the central concern of *Before and After Superflat*.
    For example, see Takashi Murakami, *Superflat, Los Angeles
    MOCA* (2001) and *Little Boy: The Art of Japan's Exploding
    Sub Cultures*, Japan Society, New York, exhibition and
    catalog (New Haven, CT: Yale University Press, 2005); and
    Yoshitomo Nara, *Nobody's Fool*, exhibition and catalog, eds.
    Melissa Chiu and Miwako Tezuka, Asia Society Museum
    (New York: Abrams, 2010).

4   Minoru Mori speaks proudly of the "artelligent city" in
    "Greetings from Roppongi Hills: The Cultural Heart of
    Tokyo," in Fumio Nanjo et al., *Art, Design and the City:
    Public Art Project 1* (Tokyo: Rikuyosha, 2004), 6–7.

5   Interviews by the author with Fram Kitagawa, June 22,
    2009, and September 30, 2014.

6   Fumio Nanjo, "Urban Strategies, Art Strategies," in Nanjo,
    Art, Design and the City, 166–71.

7   As elaborated by Charles Landry, *The Creative City: A
    Toolkit for Urban Innovators* (London: Comedia, 2000) and
    Richard Florida, *Cities and the Creative Class* (New York:
    Routledge, 2005).

8   See *Creative City Yokohama: From the Past Into the Future*
    (Yokohama, Japan: BankART 1929, 2009) and Mino Yutaka
    et al., *Encounters in the 21st Century: Polyphony—Emerging
    Resonances* (Kanazawa, Japan: 21st Century Museum of
    Contemporary Art / Tankosha, 2004).

9   Paul Waley, "Tokyo-as-World-City: Reassessing the Role
    of Capital and the State in Urban Restructuring," *Urban
    Studies* 44, no. 8 (July 2007): 1465–90 and Julian Worrall
    and Erez Golani Solomon, *21st Century Tokyo: A Guide to
    Contemporary Architecture* (Tokyo: Kodansha, 2010).

10 Roman Adrian Cybriwsky, *Roppongi Crossing: The Demise
    of a Tokyo Nightclub District and the Reshaping of a Global
    City* (Athens, Georgia: University of Georgia Press, 2010).

11 This is a typical feature of the "global city," see, for
    example, Saskia Sassen, *The Global City* (Princeton, NJ:
    Princeton University Press, 1991).

12 Jennifer Robertson, "It Takes a Village:
    Internationalization and Nostalgia in Postwar Japan,"
    in Stephen Vlastos, ed., *Mirror of Modernity: Invented
    Traditions of Modern Japan* (Berkeley: University of
    California Press, 1998), 110–31.

13 Marilyn Ivy, *Discourses of the Vanishing: Modernity,
    Phantasm, Japan* (Chicago: University of Chicago Press,
    1995).

14 Peter Matanle and Anthony Rausch with the Shrinking
    Regions Research Group, *Japan's Shrinking Regions in the
    Twenty-First Century* (Amherst, NY: Cambria Press, 2011).

15 Asato Saito, "The Politics of 'Massification' in Tokyo: The
    Causes and Consequences of Urban Re-Scaling," paper
    presented at International Sociological Association RC21
    conference, Berlin, August 29–31, 2013.

16 The founder of metabolism, Kenzō Tange, himself
    produced or oversaw several influential manifestos that
    mapped out the future of a totally urbanized Japan in the
    twenty-first century, for example, *A Plan for Tokyo* (1960),
    *Metabolism 1960: The Proposals for a New urbanism,
    presented at the World Design Conference* (1960), his
    "Tokaido Megalopolis" theory (1964), and *Japan of the
    21st Century: A Future Vision of the National Land* (1972).
    These utopian models of society are discussed by Hajime
    Yatsuka, "The Metabolism Nexus' Role in Overcoming
    Modernity," in *Metabolism: The City of the Future. Dreams
    and Visions of Reconstruction in Postwar and Present-Day
    Japan* (Tokyo: Mori Art Museum, 2011). The ideas
    were influential for the powerful LDP politician (and
    prime minister) Kakuei Tanaka, discussed later in
    the text, who published his own plan in *Remodelling
    the Japanese Archipelago* (1972).

17   Rem Koolhaas and Hans Ulrich Obrist, *Project Japan: Metabolism Talks*, ed. Kayoko Ota (Cologne: Taschen, 2011).

——

18   See Midori Yoshimoto, ed., "Expo '70 and Japanese Art: Dissonant Voices," a special edition of *Josai Review of Japanese Culture and Society* 23 (December 2011).

19   An example is *Metabolism: The City of the Future*.

——

20   Chalmers Johnson, *Miti and the Japanese Miracle: The Growth of Industrial Policy 1925–1975* (Palo Alto, CA: Stanford University Press, 1982).

21   Anthony Rausch, "The Heisei Municipal Mergers: Regional Sustainability or National Inequality?," in Stephanie Assmann, ed., *Sustainability in Post-Growth Rural Japan: Challenges and Opportunities* (London: Routledge, 2015).

——

22   I here refer to Toyo Ito's Venice Architectural Biennale prizewinning show of 2012 at the Japanese Pavilion, which imagined enlightened spatial and architectural responses to the Fukushima disasters. Toyo Ito, Kumiko Inui, Akihisa Hirata, and Naoya Hatakeyama, *Architecture. Possible Here? "Home-for-All"* (Tokyo: TOTO Publishing, 2012).

23   Shunya Yoshimi, "Radioactive Rain and the American Umbrella," *Journal of Asian Studies* 71, no. 2 (May 2012): 319–31.

——

24   In recent years there have been growing signs of an emergent civil society in Japan, albeit mostly outside the realm of conventional politics (i.e., "postpolitical" in many ways). See Jeff Kingston, *Japan's Quiet Transformation: Social Change and Civil Society in Twenty-First-Century Japan* (London: Routledge, 2004).

——

25   Raiji Kuroda, *Owarinaki kindai: Ajia bijutsu wo aruku 2009–2014* (Behind the Globalism) (Tokyo: grambooks, 2014).

26   A large collection of Fram Kitagawa's earlier writings in relation to these activities has been published by Art Front Gallery: *Kibou no bijutsu: kyoudou no yume— Kitagawa Fram no yon jyuu nen* (Art of Hope: Dreams of Collaboration—Forty Years of Fram Kitagawa) (Tokyo: Kadokawa, 2012).

27   Adrian Favell, "The Contemporary Art Market in Galapagos: Japan and the Global Art World," in Olav Velthuis and Stefano Baio-Curioni, eds., *Canvases and Careers in a Cosmopolitan Culture: On the Globalization of Contemporary Art Markets* (Oxford: Oxford University Press, 2015), 238–63.

28   Fran Lloyd, ed., *Consuming Bodies: Sex and Contemporary Japanese Art* (London: Reaktion, 2002).

——

29   Interview by the author with Yanagi's gallerist and close friend Shinichi Miyake, June 8, 2011.

30   Amelia Groom, "The Obsolete in Reverse," *Big in Japan*, October 22, 2011, http://biginjapan.com.au/2011/10/the-obsolete-in-reverse-arata-isozaki-part-one/.

31   See Ari Seligmann, "Artpolis Legacies: Proliferation of Public Architecture Programs for Urban Regeneration in Turn-of-the-Century Japan," *Proceedings of the Society of Architectural Historians*, 30th Annual Conference, Australia and New Zealand, Gold Coast, Queensland, Australia, July 2–5, 2013.

——

32   Elizabeth Norman and John Norman, "Making Decisions About Public Art: The Relevance of Community OR— Examples from Tokyo," *OR Insight* 10, no. 3 (July to September 1997): 22–26.

33   Cited in Nick West, "Public Art #4: Faret Tachikawa," *Tokyo Art Beat*, September 27, 2013, http://www.tokyoartbeat.com/tablog/entries.en/2013/09/public-art-4-faret-tachikawa.html.

——

34   Norman and Norman, "Making Decisions About Public Art," 22–26.

——

35   See Kajiya Kenji, "Art Projects in Japan: Their History and Recent Developments," *Hiroshima Art Project 2009*, exhibition catalog (Hiroshima: Japan Hiroshima City University, 2010), 261–71.

36   Interview by the author with Shingo Yamano conducted with Julian Worrall, July 30, 2012.

——

37   On Bigakko, see Yoshiko Shimada, "Gendai Shichou-Sha Bigakou," in Alice Maude-Roxby, ed., *Anti Academy*, exhibition and catalog (Southampton, England: John Hansard Gallery, 2013), 13–25; interview by the author with Yoshiko Shimada, October 1, 2014.

38 Interview by the author with Raiji Kuroda, July 4, 2013. I also owe much of my understanding about this broad history of social art in Japan to the curator Mizuki Endo (interviews on July 8, 2013, and October 27, 2013).

—

39 On Damien Hirst's legendary innovations in London with postindustrial spaces and commercial funding and publicity at *Freeze* (1988) and after, see Julian Stallabrass, *High-Art Lite: The Rise and Fall of Young British Art* (London: Verso, 1999), 50–56.

—

40 Interview by the author with Tadashi Kawamata, July 17, 2013; interview with Kawamata by Makoto Murata, Motoi Masaki, and Osamu Ikeda (1987), in *Tadashi Kawamata: Entretiens* (Paris: Editions Lutanie, 2013), 5–34.

—

41 Interview by the author with Tadashi Kawamata, July 17, 2013. See, for example, his huge Tagawa Coal Mine Project (1996–2006), developed with Yamano at an abandoned industrial site in Kyushu.

—

42 This formulation by Kawamata is discussed by Kajiya Kenji in "Art Projects in Japan" (156), in reference to a published discussion between Kawamata and Eishi Katsura in 2003.

—

43 Interview by the author with Osamu Ikeda, September 21, 2014.

—

44 Interview by the author with Tadashi Kawamata, July 17, 2013.

—

45 Interview by the author with Toyomi Hoshina, July 23, 2012; interview by the author with Masato Nakamura, April 4, 2010. I make the case for understanding Nakamura as a distinct spatial practices–based artist in *Before and After Superflat*, "Space for Our Future," 209–20.

—

46 Interview by the author with Raiji Kuroda, July 4, 2013; interview by the author with Masato Nakamura, April 4, 2010. On Beppu, see Takashi Serizawa et al., *Mixed Bathing World: Magical Property of Place and Art* (Beppu, Japan: NPO Beppu Project, 2010). Interview by the author with Tadashi Serizawa, October 28, 2013.

—

47 With thanks on this point to Peter Eckersall of CUNY, New York (meeting June 14, 2014).

—

48 See, for example, the criteria set out in Nato Thompson, ed., *Living as Form: Socially Engaged Art from 1991–2011*, exhibition and catalog (New York: MIT Press, 2012).

—

49 Yusuke Nakahara, "Portents of a Restoration in the Arts," in *Echigo-Tsumari Art Triennial*, exhibition and catalog (Tokyo: Art Front Gallery, 2000), 11–13.

—

50 See the extensive feature on this aspect of the festival in the journal of domestic architecture *Jūtaku Kenchiku* 413 (September 2009): 2–59.

—

51 For example, Lars Müller and Akiko Miki, eds., *Insular Insight: Where Art and Architecture Conspire with Nature* (Zurich: Lars Müller Publishers, 2011), which was heavily promoted with international talks, for instance at the Palais de Tokyo, Paris, December 10, 2012.

—

52 Soichiro Fukutake, "On the Closure of the Setouchi Festival 2013," in *Setouchi Triennial 2013*, exhibition and catalog (Tokyo: Bijutsu Shuppan-sha, 2014), 18–19.

—

53 Julian Worrall, interview with Soichiro Fukutake, published as "In Search of Society's True Affluence," *Japan Times*, August 20, 2010.

—

54 Yukinori Yanagi, *Inujima Note* (Tokyo: Miyake Fine Arts, 2010); Yukinori Yanagi, "Art at Large: Art Making in the Long View," artist talk, Museum of Modern Art, New York, May 3, 2013.

—

55 Fram Kitagawa, "Objectives, Status Quo and Roles of the Setouchi Festival," in *Setouchi Triennial 2013*, 20–25.

—

56 Talk by Chiharu Shiota, Japan Foundation, London, November 22, 2013.

—

57 Kitagawa, "Objectives, Status Quo and Roles of the Setouchi Festival," 20–21.

—

58 Worrall, "In Search of Society's True Affluence."

—

59 As seen in some of the mostly widely discussed survey shows in Japan since the disaster, for example: *Artists and the Disaster: Documentation in Progress*, exhibition and catalog (Mito, Japan: Art Tower Mito, 2012); *Out of Doubt*, exhibition and catalog (Tokyo: Mori Art Museum, 2013–14); *Awakening*, exhibition and catalog,

Aichi Triennale (Nagoya, Japan, 2013); and *Big Sky Friendship*, exhibition at Towada Arts Centre (April 19–September 23, 2014).

———

60   Julian Worrall, "Nature, Publicness, Place: Towards a Relational Architecture in Japan," in *Eastern Promises*, exhibition and catalog (Vienna: MAK, 2013), 93–99.

———

61   Susanne Klien, "Young Urban Migrants in the Countryside: The Quest for Purpose and Subjective Well-Being," in Stephanie Assmann, ed., *Sustainability in Contemporary Rural Japan: Challenges and Opportunities* (London: Routledge, 2015).

———

62   Susanne Klien, "Contemporary Art and Regional Revitalization: Selected Artworks in the Echigo-Tsumari Art Triennial 2000–6," *Japan Forum* 22, no. 3 (December 2010): 1–30; Susanne Klien, "Collaboration or Confrontation? Local and Non-Local Actors in the Echigo-Tsumari Art Triennial," *Contemporary Japan* 22, nos. 1 and 2 (September 2010): 1–25.

———

63   See Austin Harrington, *Art and Social Theory: Sociological Arguments in Aesthetics* (Cambridge, UK: Polity, 2004).

———

64   See Claire Bishop, "The Social Turn: Collaboration and Its Discontents," *Artforum* (February 2006): 178–83, which aroused angry debate with Kester. She then worked out her argument in a full-length book, *Artificial Hells: Participatory Art and the Politics of Spectatorship* (London: Verso, 2012). A very good guide to this debate is provided in the twin reviews by Eleanor Heartney, "Can Art Change Lives?," *Art in America* 100, no. 6 (June 12, 2012): 67–69.

———

65   This debate has centered particularly on the positions of a leading sociologist of art in Japan, Yoshitaka Mouri, and the art critic Ren Fukuzumi, who was formerly Mouri's student.

———

66   Grant Kester, *The One and the Many: Contemporary Collaborative Art in a Global Context* (Durham, NC: Duke University Press, 2011). His discussion and the ensuing debate take place in the slipstream of Nicolas Bourriaud, *Relational Aesthetics* (Paris: Les Presses du Réel, 1998).

———

67   Interviews by the author with Fram Kitagawa, June 22, 2009, and September 30, 2014.

———

68   See also Adrian Favell, "Islands for Life: Artistic Responses to Remote Social Polarization and Population Decline in Japan," in Stephanie Assmann, ed., *Sustainability in Post-Growth Rural Japan*.

———

69   A symptom of this has been the emergence of younger figures who have made significant impact on audiences as "postpolitical" guru-like radicals, articulating a thoroughgoing rejection and withdrawal from mainstream society and politics in Japan. A leading example is the young architect and cult figure Kyohei Sakaguchi, known for his Zero Yen House (2006) project, which celebrated the low-cost, sustainable self-sufficiency with which the homeless manage to build houses for themselves in the margins of the big city. After the 3.11 disaster he created his own alternative "Zero Republic" in Kumamoto for those wishing to reject mainstream economic and political values, "seceding" from the mainland and declaring himself "president." A similar figure, Hiroshi Ito, based in Wakayama, has published popular self-help books about how young NEET (not in employment, education, or training) or the working poor can opt out and re-create self-sufficient and fulfilling lives in remote locations far from the city, for example, his *Furusato wo tsukuru* (Making a Hometown) (Tokyo: Shoseki, 2014).

———

70   There are, however, the beginnings of debate about "post-Bubble urbanism" in China. See, for example, the special edition of *Urban China* 68 (January 2015), to which I contributed a piece about postgrowth art and architecture in Japan: "Islands for Life: Artistic Responses in Post-Bubble Japan": 90–93.

Chapter 06

Collaborations That Transcend Regionality, Generations, and Professions

Art Is Like a Baby

110 Takamasa Kuniyasu (Japan), *The Seat of Rain Spirit* and *Matsudai Dragon Pagoda*, 2000–2009

Projects that begin with opposition and criticism can develop with the involvement of the local residents. Takamasa Kuniyasu's work is a perfect example. Created for the first triennial, *The Seat of Rain Spirit* was an image of the dragon god of agriculture and rice production descending to a sacred place. Kuniyasu used coppiced wood and planned to build this structure on his own. Occasionally, he had university students assist him by stacking and binding the pieces, but he had difficulty securing them. When some of the local community members were making fun of him, Kuniyasu asked, "You want to try?" The elderly villagers took up the challenge and helped the artist complete the piece, which couldn't, ultimately, have been done alone. At that moment, the dragon god left the artist and became part of the locals.

The dragon spirit was initially intended to be up for just fifty days, but once the time period was over, no one sought to dismantle it. It lasted through another triennial before fear of it collapsing from the harsh weather and earthquakes made it necessary to take it down. The locals wanted to rebuild another one in 2006. Even the Tokamachi fire crew wanted to assist, and they constructed an even larger form, which is the *Matsudai Dragon Pagoda*.

The elderly villagers told visitors the story about how the sculpture came to be.

Art is like a baby. It can be cumbersome and burdensome and will perish if left alone. Perhaps that is why it is necessary to seek the support of those around it to help nourish it. The dragon spirit is the reflection of such cooperation and collaboration.

Locals helping construct the *Dragon Pagoda*

Construction of the earthen walls

Collaborations That Transcend Regionality, Generations, and Professions

111 Hiroshi Furugori (Japan), *Bonkei-II / Archetype Landscape II*, 2003

Hiroshi Furugori has participated in the triennial since its inauguration. In preparation for the second edition, he wanted to create gigantic fort-like earthen walls in a rice field. When the Gejo district asked to work with an artist who could create "work that is powerful," I introduced Furugori without hesitation.

Back when I was running around to explain and convince community members to participate in the triennial, Gejo was one of the two communities that first agreed to host artworks in their settlements. (The other one was Hachi.) Given all the opposition from elsewhere, I was greatly encouraged by their attitudes. Gejo has distinguished itself in Echigo-Tsumari in terms of its cooperative attitude, power, and solidarity.

Two terraced rice fields of Gejo that were not in use that year were prepared as a site. The plan was to combine the clay from the rice fields with straw and wood to construct earthen walls using a traditional method. The production seemed to progress slowly, even with the opening date looming. Three weeks from the deadline, it was barely half complete, and yet Furugori was unfazed.

The concerned members of Gejo made an announcement to all locals after consultations: "Until the opening, all adults will utilize paid leave time as much as possible to assist. Children shall rush to the site immediately after school to assist." During those three weeks, it rained most of the time. But they built the wall by laying a mat and planks along the hill, contending with the slippery mud. They were even able to build another wall in the higher terraced field, which was beyond the goals of the original plan for *Bonkei-II*. The traditional farming work ethic connected with the artist's desire to build and construct.

The results are striking earthen walls that stand side by side, surrounded by lush green terraced rice fields. The reputation of the work spread like wildfire, and more than fifty thousand visitors went to see it. In preparation for rice planting for the next spring and heavy snow season, the work had to be removed at the end of the festival season. It was painful for the people of Gejo, and they held a ceremony to return the artwork back to the earth.

112

112 Kidlat Tahimik (Philippines),
Postwar Love letter: To Niigata Rice Terraces from Ifugao Rice Terraces, with Love, 2009–12
Kidlat Tahimik grew up in an elite household in the Philippines. One day, he abruptly quit his job at the OECD in Paris and became a documentary filmmaker. He moved to Ifugao, as he was interested in the indigenous Filipino cultures there. During World War II, Ifugao was caught up in warfare. It is also a UNESCO World Heritage Site for its terraced rice fields. During the fourth triennial, Tahimik proposed transporting and reconstructing an Ifugao hut and an accompanying tribe as a demonstration of cultural exchange between two communities and two countries that share a strong culture of rice terracing.

It proved extremely difficult to immigrate a tribe of twenty people. We made various attempts, to no avail, and I finally emailed Tahimik that we should abandon the idea. He responded, "This is not a work of 'art for art's sake,' nor an anthropological study. This is a significant intercultural exchange between village and village, artists and artists, country and country." He went on, explaining the context of historical exchanges between Japan and the Philippines, more historical examples from World War II, and arrived at the conclusion that he was composing a "love letter" from Ifugao that sought an understanding and acceptance of the landowners and communities of Niigata. I was moved by this. Despite continued challenges concerning immigration and the hosting site, we worked hard to process immigration papers, raised funds, and established a host site at Gejo village. The residents of Gejo embraced the visitors with open arms and the hut was established at the terraced field. Since then, the people of Gejo have traveled to visit the people of Ifugao in the Philippines, and the Ifugao people returned to Echigo-Tsumari in 2012, continuing a rich exchange.

113

113 Kimio Tsuchiya (Japan),
Creative Garden, 2009–ongoing
Highway 253 is an artery from Tokamachi, and there are
many tunnels, which make travel and communication
between the distinct cultural zones of Tokamachi and
Matsudai far easier; before they were dug, it was unheard
of for one villager to see another from a different village.
Along this highway, approaching Matsudai, is a crescent-
shaped flower garden. Kimio Tsuchiya, the residents,
and the Kohebi Volunteers completed this garden for the
second festival.

The proposal played on how the formerly windy, snaking
roads had been cut straight through, leaving an empty,
pocket-shaped space at the intersection between the
former and the new road. Permission to make it a park was
requested repeatedly from the Niigata Prefecture, and after
a year it was finally received. The pocket park plan began in
1999 and took much longer than anticipated. Engineering
work began in July 2002 after site research and numerous
Tsuchiya workshops involving local residents. In May 2003,

just before the opening of the second triennial, more than
a hundred fifty people, including the local residents, local
government, and the Kohebi Volunteers, planted twelve
thousand flowers, and a beautiful garden was realized.

Putting on a triennial demands many steps and much
patience. Long negotiations put pressure on those who are
heavily invested and involved. Because this was an effort
from the ground up, it serves as an example of the "epoch
making strategy" and now serves as a model for others.

The twenty elderly residents who participated in this
activity refer to themselves as the Matsudai Scarecrow
Corps. Now organized, they continue to be active in a
variety of projects in Echigo-Tsumari, and particularly
in Matsudai NOHBUTAI. My heart warms when I see the
members guiding visitors, for free, with great enthusiasm.

118

114, 115 Yuko Matsuzawa (Japan), *Enishi,* 2009
An installation composed of 170,000 pins connected by fisherman's knots forms a spiderweb hanging above a field of pins on the floor of the former Akakura Elementary School gymnasium. Yuko Matsuzawa lived in the school for three months to complete this work. The members of the settlement donated rice balls and volunteered their time. More than four hundred participants helped to complete the work. The title, *Enishi,* suggests *en,* or fate/ties, a significant aspect of this work. The picture shows women in their nineties, eighties, seventies, and sixties working together.

116, 117 Sue Pedley (Australia), *Haze,* 2006
Patterns inspired by the local dress and tools were sewn onto Australian wool by members of the settlement and Kohebi Volunteers. These were then hung on the haze, which is used for drying rice. Rice farmers easily accomplished this familiar task.

———

118 Kazunari Nitta (Japan), *White Project,* 2003
The white cloth made by members of the community was joined to represent the connection between the spirits of people, the world, and generations. Many of the elderly, children from the community, and Kohebi Volunteers contributed to the quilting of 12,215 white pieces of clothing.

Public Works and Art

119 Casagrande & Rintala Architectural Office (Finland), *Potemkin*, 2003–ongoing

Rather than seeing public art as simply placing sculptures outdoors, there is a move toward approaching art as a public works project. This is a strategy that has led to many permanent installations at the triennial. *Potemkin* by the architectural office of Casagrande & Rintala, Richard Deacon's *Mountain* (2006–ongoing), and Dominique Perrault's *Pavillon / Papillon* (2006–ongoing) are examples. *Potemkin* is a model that is particularly memorable for me. The site for this project is near the river within the Kuramata settlement in a location that suffered industrial waste dumping. I felt that this would be a good site to match with Casagrande & Rintala.

This project was proposed as one of the Niigata Prefecture's Pocket Park Projects. Casagrande & Rintala went beyond the conventional public park designed by some local construction company. Instead of simply plopping playground equipment and sculptures on the site, the firm wanted to be involved from the beginning and realize a park as art with public money, while maintaining the necessary elements of a public park.

The site was covered with thickets and garbage. Casagrande & Rintala resolved to minimize the elements of the park and use Corten steel walls as a way to establish a meditative space. The designers spent several months carefully considering the height of the walls, the thickness of the steel, and whether or not to incorporate a sauna (an idea they gave up on). They also received considerable support from the local residents, who helped clean up trash and fed them while they worked on site. The project gained momentum as an example of a public works art project with the implication of sustainability through the support and the commitment of the community.

When the work was nearly completed, Casagrande & Rintala came to the site with university students from Finland, Norway, France, Alaska, and Puerto Rico to host workshops. They built wooden benches together and *Potemkin* was completed.

When you enter *Potemkin*, there is a "junkyard garden" made of dead trees and industrially recycled glass pebbles. The space opens up to a white garden where a dozen trees stand. The space is reminiscent of a postindustrial Ryoan-ji temple or Ginkaku-ji temple, but it can be walked on and thus spatially and texturally experienced under one's feet. Travel to the back end of the rock garden, and there is a cottagelike structure made of Corten steel, where the murmuring of the river can be enjoyed as your mood softens. A fortlike partition creates a separation from the rice fields, designed to direct one's consciousness toward the river in the back. I get the sense that this park is designed to function as a rhythmic and lyrical metaphor for the movement of people and the opening up of the senses, making it a place one wants to visit again.

Top: Casagrande & Rintala and the students at work
Bottom: View of the park

The Transformation of Disaster Relief to Noh Stage Pavilion

120 Dominique Perrault (France), *Pavillon / Papillon,* 2006–ongoing

While planning the third edition, we decided we wanted to build a pavilion in the Shinmei Waterfront Park, taking advantage of available support for reconstruction projects following the Chūetsu Earthquake in Niigata Prefecture. The Gejo district community had been very supportive from the first triennial on, and they agreed to let us expand their cherished park.

The park was located near the epicenter and was destroyed during the earthquake. There was road damage, waterline damage, and collapsed houses, in addition to landslides that bared the surface of the mountainside park. The architect Dominique Perrault was invited to build a quiet pavilion in front of the pond.

Perrault was only thirty-five years old when he was awarded the commission for the National Library of France, and he completed the translucent design, consisting of four buildings, in 1995. Known for his postmodern approach, he also won the competition to design the Mariinsky Theater in Saint Petersburg, Russia, in 2003. At first glance, his career may appear to be incongruous with a design for a small pavilion, but I was intrigued by the possibilities.

I flew to France to interview him. I said, "You are currently working on one of the world's most renowned and largest theaters in Saint Petersburg. Next would you like to come to a rural village in

121

Echigo-Tsumari to make the world's smallest theater?" Perrault agreed, and the *Pavillon / Papillon* remains one of the smallest projects he has done to date.

For the opening of the third triennial, the *Tsumari Kanze Noh Play* was performed. This performance was a prayer for recovery from the earthquake and was produced by Keiichiro Tsuchiya. The *kyogen* performance *Sado-gitsune* (Fox of Sado Island, Niigata) by Yukio Ishida and the Noh play *Hagoromo* (Feather Mantle) by Kiyokazu Kanze, the twenty-sixth headmaster of the Kanze School, were played out in front of the audience. The mirrored roof of various angles reflected the performers, water, and greenery. The effect was surreal, and the audience appreciated the harmony between humans and nature.

—

121 Tsumari Kanze, *Noh: Prayer for Recovery from the Great Chūetsu Earthquake*, 2006

125

126

Turning Roads, Parking Lots, and Bathrooms into Art

122 Richard Deacon (UK), *Mountain,* 2006–ongoing
Richard Deacon installed a silver tube sculpture
in a parking lot as a bench. One can enjoy the view
of Mount Kurohime over this complex tubular form.
There are also benches nearby constructed out of the
same material.

123 R&Sie Sarl d'Architecture (France),
Asphalt Spot, 2003–ongoing
The outdoor exhibition space is built into a parking lot
with bathroom stalls. The twisted blacktop is part
of the terrain and creates a sense of continuity with the
existing road. The undulations in black and white relate
to the mountains in view.

124 Hiromi Ashitaka (Japan), *Passage,* 2006–ongoing
Ashitaka created a bench with seventy legs at the bus
stop near Kawanishi High School. Carved into it are
words students created in workshops.

125 CLIP (Japan),
Lanterns in the Ravine, 2000–ongoing
The entrance to the Matsunoyama Onsen district
is equipped with structures functioning as sign,
restroom, bathroom, etc. Like a traditional lantern of
a tavern, it invites people to visit this sacred hot spring
and has become a landmark.

126 Jiro Ogawa / Ogawa Laboratory, Nippon Institute of
Technology (Japan), *Mud Men,* 2006–ongoing
Standing by the river, this small folly is composed
of human forms modeled on the residents of the
community. It is made from a concrete clay
composite material.

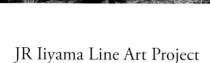

JR Iiyama Line Art Project

The JR railway line that connects Nagano Prefecture with Niigata Prefecture is the Iiyama Line. The JR Iiyama Line Art Project was launched at the fifth triennial to expand art to stations with the aim of deepening exchanges between visitors from cities and the local residents. We envisioned the station as a "port" bringing visitors to the communities and nature.

There are ten stations in this area; the ones that implemented the project in 2012 included Gejo Station and Echigo-Tazawa Station. In addition, there was another project in which the train itself served as the canvas for artist Jean-Michel Alberola. Throughout Japan, the local lines have few users because of depopulation and the general preference for using cars, given the sprawling landscape. This causes concern for the line's continued economic sustainability. In Echigo-Tsumari, visitors and tourists use cars, and the downturn continues. This project focuses on the railway as a stage or site for discourse.

127 Jean-Michel Alberola (France),
      Aller Retour, 2012
      The artist drew people's faces on this yellow train,
      which runs the Iiyama Line between Echigo-Kawaguchi
      Station and Morimiyanohara Station. Messages on it
      say, "Why don't you try talking to them again?" or
      "If you walk, then the sky and earth say hello!"

      ———

      MIKAN and Kanagawa University Sogabe Lab (Japan),
      Gejo Thatch Tower, 2012–ongoing
      The team created a thatched-roof tower forty feet high
      and about thirty square feet in area at Gejo Station
      housing old farm equipment and furniture and
      functioning as a micro museum of agriculture. This
      area is known for craftsmen of thatched roofs. Proposed
      as part of the Iiyama Line Art Project, the tower has
      become a symbol of the station.

128 Atelier Bow-Wow and Tsukamoto Lab, Tokyo Institute
      of Technology (Japan), *Boat Shed,* 2012–ongoing
      This work is a long, skinny structure built alongside the
      platform of the Echigo-Tazawa station. It houses the
      work of Tatsuo Kawaguchi. The interior is filled with
      natural light. This house is connected to the station
      plaza and serves as the starting point of exchanges
      between the region and cities.

      ———

129 Tatsuo Kawaguchi (Japan), *Voyage to the Future;*
      Waterborne Canes of the Heart, 2012–ongoing
      This piece, in which countless seeds cover the fishing
      boat on display at the *Boat Shed,* is entitled *Voyages to the*
      Future. The back room has a water tank that fills with
      groundwater and many canes that appear to be hovering.
      It makes us think of the root of the land's life force
      and its future.

James Turrell's Artwork: A House You Can Stay In

130 James Turrell (USA), *House of Light*, 2000–ongoing

The *House of Light* was created in the former Kawanishi town, known for plains that allow one to look out at the sky, unlike the rest of Echigo-Tsumari. There was a public work project to develop cottages and campgrounds, and I felt strongly that I would like artists to be involved. I was interested in cottages that could be regarded as artworks, but also accommodate lodgers.

The announcement of James Turrell's Roden Crater project in Arizona was major news in the art world. The work is a crater that he has carved into a sort of gigantic observatory. When it is completed, it will be the world's largest land art project. I went to Arizona to meet Turrell.

We spoke while lying in the bottom of a crater. There was no up or down; left and right were indistinguishable. Light was something that could connect humans with the faraway. This was truly a surreal way to share time with the artist. When he agreed to create a work for the Echigo-Tsumari project, there was one condition, which was that it needed to be a place where viewers could stay overnight. In this way, they would experience the dawn and the sun setting. To have such a famous artist was a budgetary challenge, but we settled on the proposal for the *House of Light* instead of building four cottages.

The details of the building are modeled after the residence of Hoshina, who has been the grand landowner here since the Edo period. It is situated on a hill overlooking the Shinano River and Tokamachi. The second floor consists of the dining room and living room, and the first floor houses the bathrooms and bedrooms. The second-floor roof slides open to expose a skylight window where one can watch the sky and its changing light. There is also carefully curated lighting in the floors and in the bathroom, where fiber-optic lights create an illusory effect. A sublime sky show and details of light within the house are a spectacular exhibition that can only be experienced by those who lodge there.

130

The change of light at sunset

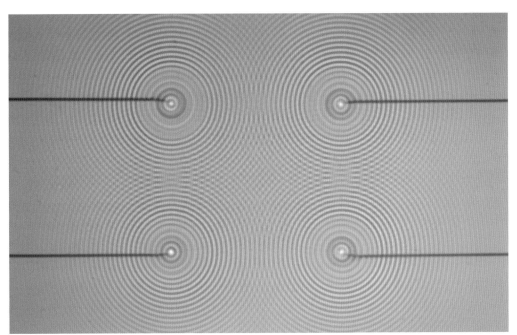

136

137

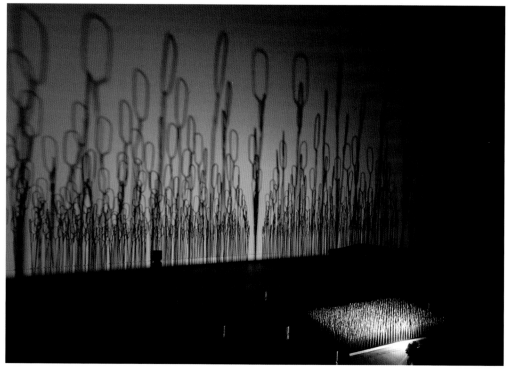

Museum as a Gateway: The Echigo-Tsumari Satoyama Museum of Contemporary Art, KINARE

The KINARE was first created in 2003; a major renovation was completed in 2012. Both the construction and the renovation were aimed at creating a place that symbolizes and reflects the characteristics and uniqueness of Echigo-Tsumari. Once the museum was established, our vision became ever clearer. The architect Hiroshi Hara's original concept was a nomadic community-caravan that would gather around an oasis in the desert.

The art tour around the *satoyama* becomes a journey in which one discovers the charms and diversity of the various settlements. KINARE is walking distance from the Tokamachi Station, which welcomes the JR Iiyama Line and the Hokuetsu Express Hokuhoku Line. It is one of the triennial sites and is regarded as the gateway to the Echigo-Tsumari experience. It could also be viewed as the final stop of one's journey, to reassess what one has seen or wants to see in the future. In this way, it serves many roles.

During the time of the 2003 triennial, KINARE took advantage of its semioutdoor corridor, which is a large open space unusual in the snow country, for a variety of markets called *rakuichi-rakuza*. With its second-floor traditional crafts zone, its corridor made a great impact on the locality, which was suffering a "hollowing out" as people migrated to the city. Many temporary participatory artworks were installed, which attracted not only visitors from outside but also local residents. But the visitorship decreased after that, and the city of Tokamachi requested that we renew it as a facility fully incorporating contemporary art.

In 2012, the remodeling of the museum coincided with the fifth triennial. The museum was one of the special featured works that since the beginning had helped visitors visualize the region, just as the Matsudai Snow-Land Agrarian Culture Center is nested together with the art sites in the neighboring Joyama. KINARE is intended to help envision and experience the complexity of the world—the contemporaneity, communities, and *satoyama*.

The subjects addressed by the thirteen artworks that are part of the permanent collection are the Shinano River, Echigo clay, deciduous trees, settlements, landscape, tunnels, Jomon vessels, snow, and more. In other words, these works are site-specific in terms of reflecting distinct characteristics of Echigo-Tsumari. Here the metaphor of the nesting boxes is explored by the design of the architect Hiroshi Hara. The square is a pure geometric form that contrasts the complex cityscape and grounds. The use of concrete and glass creates a silent presence, achieving an otherworldly feel. The interior is like a nesting box, with rooms inside other rooms. The artworks installed there modularly nest together, and the viewer recognizes that the world is embedded in one region, as the Japanese archipelago is embedded in Echigo-Tsumari.

131 Hiroshi Hara and Atelier Φ (Japan),
Echigo-Tsumari Satoyama Museum of Contemporary
Art, KINARE, 2003–ongoing
KINARE was designed as a tentlike structure, recalling
places where nomadic caravans would come to an
oasis and open free markets. It opened in 2003 as
a community cultural exchange center, and nine years
later, in 2012, it was renovated as a contemporary art
museum, which houses a collection based on
local themes and organizes temporary exhibitions
year-round.
—

132 Gerda Steiner and Jörg Lenzlinger (Switzerland), *Ghost Satellites,* 2012–ongoing
The artists imagined Echigo-Tsumari as a satellite far
off from the center of Japan. They constructed this
work with found objects that they collected while
staying here. They created thirty-three satellites, which
they gave historical satellite names. They are exhibited
at the entrance of the museum.
—

133 Leandro Erlich (Argentina), *Tunnel,* 2012–ongoing
Many tunnels and semicylinder-shaped storehouses
can be seen while driving through Echigo-Tsumari.
These two mundane objects were combined to form
a disorienting installation.
—

134 Carlos Garaicoa (Cuba), *Fuyu,*
2012–ongoing
Silver bits of paper cut into shapes of typical houses
and buildings of Echigo-Tsumari are housed inside
a glass case. They are blown around within the box,
shimmering and falling like snow. Viewers who
experience the inside of this installation are enveloped
in silver snowflakes and the community of Echigo-
Tsumari.
—

135 Koji Yamamoto (Japan), *Phlogiston,* 2012–ongoing
This is a forest of eighteen kinds of deciduous trees
from the region that have been fired and carbonized.
The objects are displayed on pedestals that are stumps
of the trees that were used to create the objects.
—

136 Carsten Nicolai (Germany),
Wellenwanne LFO, 2012–ongoing
The image on the screen shows radial waves
responding to the frequency of sounds. The strobe
lighting on the ceiling passes through the water
and reflects the image that captures the essence
of Shinano River: water, wave, and resonance.

137 Jomon Vessel
—

138 Carsten Höller (Belgium/Sweden),
Rolling Cylinder 2012, 2012–ongoing
The artist was inspired by red, white, and blue barber
signs. A rotating tube of colors surrounds viewers,
causing disorientation while awakening new physical
senses and consciousness.
—

139 Ryota Kuwakubo (Japan), *LOST #6,* 2012–ongoing
A model railway travels slowly through the darkness
as if moving through Echigo-Tsumari. Tools and
pieces of looms are lit up and cast shadows within
the room. The shadows appear to be a landscape or
scenery that impresses upon the viewer a feeling of
déjà vu and *jamais vu.*
—

140 Elmgreen & Dragset (Denmark, Norway/Germany),
Powerless Structures, Fig. 429, 2012–ongoing
The quintessential twentieth-century
"white cube" gallery space is stacked to create a sense
of tension. The light from the windows flickers like
emergency vehicles. These are critical cubes installed in
a new museum.
—

141 Massimo Bartolini featuring Lorenzo Bini (Italy),
○ *in* □, 2012–ongoing
This piece is composed of bookshelves in the shape
of an arch, circular tables and chairs, and mobiles
hanging from the ceiling. When the tables are
connected, the drawings featured on them represent
the Shinano River. A light fixture resembles clouds,
and the circular mobiles are inspired by refracted
light. By embedding various types of circles in a
square building, the artists designed the interior space
as a work that inspires the visitor to experience the
relationship between humans and nature based on the
theme of the Shinano River.

The Essence of the Echigo-Tsumari Experience: The Matsudai Snow-Land Agrarian Culture Center NOHBUTAI

Central to the Matsudai Station of the Hokuhoku line are the highway tunnels that sandwich the narrow, flat plains where a shopping arcade has been a gathering place for people since long ago. When you pass the railway toward Joyama hill, there are farms and rice fields. Echigo-Tsumari proposed this to be the site of a field museum that would spread over the area, and at its core would be the Matsudai Snow-Land Agrarian Culture Center NOHBUTAI.

I searched throughout Japan and also abroad for an architect who could plan this in preparation for the first triennial. I needed someone who could navigate the details of planning for a site near the station, under the high-tension wire, safe from snow vehicles. I approached the Dutch office of MVRDV. We submitted the firm's proposals to the municipal government. The government felt that it lacked "Japanese-ness." Two years later, we resubmitted it, and it was accepted.

There were additional conditions that had overwhelmed the previous attempt, such as preserving Kabakov's field theater, and that the bottom of the structure needed space underneath for events in the winter, as well as galleries, a restaurant space, and artist spaces. All this needed to be considered. MVRDV joyfully collected and considered all of those conditions, as NOHBUTAI was the first project the firm had embarked on outside of Europe.

There are approximately fifty works installed around this building and the nearby Joyama hill. The impressive number and quality of the works in this one area led other areas to complain that it is unfair that Matsudai had so many artworks. The generous decision of the mayor of Matsudai at the first triennial played a role in how this happened. At the time, we were planning 140 works of art in Echigo-Tsumari but concerns about the budget led to most of the municipalities wanting fewer pieces, if possible. Matsudai accepted a considerable portion of the work. Today its collection of artworks has become the most important property of the area.

I would like to restate the NOHBUTAI concept at this point. Any person believes that the place they are in is the center of the world and that one's personal environment is a microcosm of the world. The microcosm of Japan is Niigata Prefecture and, if Niigata's microcosm is Echigo-Tsumari, then NOHBUTAI is the compressed version of the world of Echigo-Tsumari. There was a sense of wanting to capture the feel of mountainous Japan-ness. This is why we worked to cultivate the essence of Echigo-Tsumari and thereby the essence of our world to be experienced in this place of NOHBUTAI, even if one stays for only a few hours.

NOHBUTAI activities gain value by representing the regional farming and traditional way of life as a potential model for the world beyond. The museum hosts workshops in terraced rice field management and farming techniques.

146 | 147 | 148

151

152

142 MVRDV, Matsudai Snow-Land Agrarian Culture Center
NOHBUTAI, 2003–ongoing
The white building stands on four legs, seeming to float
atop the rice paddies. Each room is carefully considered
and houses artwork; offers a space for food, shopping,
and events; and even provides workshops for visitors to
experience farming culture. There is a rocky landscape
on the rooftop.

———

143 Jean-Luc Vilmouth (France),
Cafe Reflet, 2003–ongoing
Jean-Luc Vilmouth installed one hundred disposable
cameras in the windows of homes and had residents
photograph landscapes from there. After one year,
the photographs were collected and mounted on four
round light fixture ceiling displays, grouped into four
seasons. The daily lives of the residents are reflected
on mirrored tables in the restaurant. Guests enjoy the
cuisine made of local ingredients while viewing the
images of the community reflected on the table and the
terraced rice fields from the window.

———

144 Fabrice Hybert (France), *Autour du Feu,*
Dans le Desert, 2003–ongoing
This space was designed around a hearth, and people
can gather on benches. The walls have one-centimeter
holes throughout, where the light streams in. These
organic 1,001 holes reference the *1,001 Arabian Nights,*
thus referring in part to the American involvement
in Iraq at that time. One contemplates the meaning
of living in his or her place by imagining what is
happening in another place on Earth.

———

145 Tatsuo Kawaguchi (Japan), *Relation—Blackboard*
Classroom, 2003–ongoing
The artist covered the entirety of the interior of a
classroom in blackboards. The walls, floor, ceiling, table,
and even maps and the globe can be drawn on with
chalk.

———

146 Tsuyoshi Ozawa (Japan),
Kamaboko-Type Storehouse Project, 2003–ongoing
The artist was inspired by the local semicircular roofed
(*kamaboko*-type) storehouses. He found interesting
the fact that they are made of tubes used for the tunnel
drilling work of the Hokuhoku line. Fish-eye lenses
were installed in the storehouses, allowing visitors to
look inside. The seven storehouses are all different
in size, which affects the shape of the snow that
accumulates on the roofs.

147 Josep-Maria Martin (Spain), *Museum of the Constellation*
Families of Matsudai, 2003–ongoing
Fifteen hundred colored bars connect the Matsudai station
with NOHBUTAI. Each Matsudai resident selected a color
and had his or her house name written on it. There is also
a video monitor installed at the end of the path that
streams images of residents welcoming visitors.

———

148 Hiroko Inoue (Japan),
Memory-Regeneration, 2003–ongoing
This work stacks boulders in a gentle arc within an oval
shape. Each boulder was inscribed with the name of
someone significant to the local residents and then placed
on the soil. Even if the names were to disappear, the act
of joining in the project would remain in the residents'
memories.

———

149 Shintaro Tanaka (Japan), *The ○△□ Tower*
and the Red Dragonfly, 2000–ongoing
This landmark takes the form of a red dragonfly sculpture
forty-six feet high. It is a symbol of spiritual homeland for
both the people who live in the *satoyama* landscape and
those in the cities.

———

150 Pascale Marthine Tayou (Cameroon/Belgium),
Reversed City, 2009–ongoing
Each of the gigantic pencils shows the names of various
countries. The work is elevated six feet from the ground.
The viewer looks up at the colorful pencils hung from
above, pointing to the viewers, and the sensation is of both
dynamism and threat.

———

151 Christian Lapie (France), *Fort 61,* 2000–ongoing
Charred wooden sculptures are installed on the hill of the
Matsudai castle ruin. The figurative works and spherical
forms evoke a serene mood.

———

152 Menashe Kadishman (Israel), *Trees,* 2000–ongoing
A symbol of a tree is cut from a standing steel plane.
The negative space of the representation of nature
demands attention.

———

153 Tobias Rehberger (Germany),
Fichte (Fir tree), 2003–ongoing
In Germany, the metaphor for literature and philosophy is
a deep forest. The library inside the forest is a collection of
German literature translated into Japanese. The books were
collected in cooperation with publishing companies and the
Goethe Institut Tokyo.

154 Hermann Maier Neustadt (Germany),
WD Spiral Part III Magic Theatre, 2003–ongoing
The three cylindrical sculptures are large enough for
viewers to walk into. The trees and grass from outside
are seen through the semitransparent walls made of
acrylic and FRP, and are reflected, along with the viewer,
in the mirrored walls and ceiling.

—

155 Périphériques (France),
Matsudai Small Tower, 2003–ongoing
From the top of the observatory, one can view the town
through a cedar grove. This four-story work is located
in a campsite and constructed out of steel pipes and
metal mesh.

—

156 Yung Ho Chang and Atelier FCJZ (China),
Rice House, 2003–ongoing
This is a space to relax and enjoy the view of
a rice field.

—

157 Simon Beer (Switzerland),
Carpe Diem, 2000–ongoing
Six snowmen created with children from Matsudai are
stored in six refrigerators built in a pavilion with a red
roof. The snowmen symbolize the six areas of Echigo-
Tsumari. After the exhibition, we let them melt to
return them to the field.

—

158 Tatsuji Ushijima (Japan), *Observatory,* 2000–ongoing
The sounds above and below can be heard as you bring
your ears against the openings. The vertical voice tubes
bring the sounds of the earth to one ear and the sounds
of the sky to the other. One has to walk on a path
between rice paddies to experience the work.

—

159 Masayuki Hashimoto (Japan),
Under a Cedar in Snow Country, 2000–ongoing
This work was inspired by the roots of trees that
bend from the weight of snow. It is expected to be
incorporated into the forest in the future.

—

160 Shigeyo Kobayashi (Japan) *They came down as if
they were photosynthesizing time: Three vulnerable
kinds of Red Data plants,* 2000–ongoing
The sculpture is a representation of snow,
inspired by the three kinds of plants in Niigata
that are endangered.

CLIP (Japan), *Walkway,* 2000–ongoing
CLIP created the pattern of movement around NOHBUTAI.
The paths connecting the artworks scattered through the
area have been designed for people to use farm roads,
mountain passes, and existing footpaths to protect the
ecology of the region.

—

161 Mio Shirai (Japan),
Restaurant Gives Orders, 2000–ongoing
Eight brightly colored doors articulate space, inspired by
Kenji Miyazawa's story "The Restaurant of Many Orders."
The guest passes through the doors according to the
orders painted on them and feels lost in the world of
a narrative.

—

162 Izumi Tachiki (Japan), *Pool of Water,* 2000–ongoing
A *suikinkutsu,* or water harp cave (a buried earthen
jar that makes a sound when water drips into it), is
installed in an abandoned rice terrace. Water drops make
subtle sounds in the cave. The work refers in part to the
importance of water in maintaining rice fields.

—

163 Madan Lal (India), *Peace Garden,* 2000–ongoing
Bud-like sculptures are placed alongside a small
pond. The sculptures are constructed out of a soft marble
from India. The lotus is a symbol of Brahman, one of the
Hindu gods.

—

164 Noriko Yanagisawa (Japan), *Toru,* 2003–ongoing
The artist was inspired by the landscape to install a saucer-
like object to represent the local people's anticipation of
spring. Fifteen thousand pieces of marble are inlaid in a
mosaic relief. The motifs on the relief show wings, mineral
ores, and tree ammonites, which reference the ancient
memory of humans. The irregularly shaped chairs also
suggest fragments of the ammonite.

Every Resident Is a Scientist:
Echigo-Matsunoyama Museum of Natural Science, Kyororo

The juror is a crucial part of a competition. I always try to invite the most interesting artists and architects as jurors. This is why when I thought about the Kyororo museum, whose name was inspired by the cry of the indigenous Asian kingfisher, I requested Jun Aoki, Kazuhiro Kojima, and Kazuyo Sejima as the jurors.

Kyororo was part of the four stages of art festival planning and had one of the clearest missions. I wanted to highlight the wisdom and experience of the local people and explore it as science of real life, as opposed to lab-based scientific research. With the mission statement "Every resident is a scientist," I invited the astrophysicist Satoru Ikeuchi to be the supervisor.

There were an astounding number of applicants for this contest. The building had to take into consideration the ecology of the region and the functions of a science museum, and had to withstand the weight of snow during the winter. Eventually, the plan by Takaharu Tezuka and Yui Tezuka was selected; their design for the observatory was for it to be buried in snow and appear to be an underwater submarine. They proposed that the entire structure would be constructed out of Corten steel, which expands and contracts by as much as eight inches between summer and winter.

In addition to the science pavilion equipment, various artworks were permanently installed. Taking the theme "art without form," they were integrated into the building. Toshikatsu Endo created a work to sense the water under your feet; Yasuko Shono made a device to listen to the sounds of spring water falling into a well; Takuro Osaka turned a shower of cosmic rays into lights.

When Endo said he wanted to make a huge aquarium out of steel in the courtyard, there was strong opposition. At the last meeting, I was asked, Kitagawa, did you feel the sense of water on the steel plate when you were on Endo's piece in Hakone? I replied, no, unfortunately not, and everyone laughed at my response. They said, I appreciate your honesty, and somehow we gained permission to build *Water Under Foot, 200m³*. However, when the Chūetsu Earthquake happened in 2004, people could hear the *chappon chappon* sounds coming from Endo's piece and at that point, everyone was able to confirm the sense of water.

Kyororo science pavilion also has an amazing butterfly collection donated by Usuke Shiga, an entomologist from Matsunoyama. Surrounding it are two hundred acres of beautiful *satoyama*, where Jenny Holtzer's artwork serves as signposts identifying the path. Three doctoral scientists are selected for participation during each three-year term, and they organize environmental research workshops and *satoyama* preservation activities. It was selected as a model area of the Support Project for the Study of Science & Technology (fostering the next generation of leaders in these fields) by the Japan Science and Technology Agency. There are repeat visitors from the big cities too. Through trial and error, Kyororo has hosted a variety of activities, and this path has led Kyororo to a place in the vanguard.

165 Takaharu and Yui Tezuka, Tezuka Architects (Japan),
Echigo-Matsunoyama Museum of Natural Science,
Kyororo, 2003–ongoing
The path leading to the museum takes a snakelike form.
Treetops can be observed from the 112-foot-tall tower.
During the winter, when the museum is mostly buried
in snow, visitors are guided by the snow walls until
suddenly, there's the entrance. All the windows are thick
acrylic, and in the summer, visitors see a wall of trees
and rice terraces. In the winter, they look out onto
a cross-section of snow.

—

166 Toshikatsu Endo (Japan),
Water Under Foot, 200m³, 2003–ongoing
From the entrance to the courtyard of the steel
structure, you are walking over water for more
than two hundred yards. You cannot see the
water level, because it is hidden by steel, but you
imagine its presence.

167 Norihisa Hashimoto + scope (Japan),
*Super high-resolution human-sized
photographs—life-size*, 2006–ongoing
The artist photographed local insects over
the course of a year and enlarged their scale to
that of humans. It is possible to see details
that are invisible with the naked eye.
The photographs emphasize the beauty
and diversity of insect forms.

—

168 Jenny Holzer (USA),
Nature Walk, 2003–ongoing
The hiking path connected to the Kyororo has
inscribed stones. The 102 rocks installed along
the mile-long path guide and speak to the viewer.

169

Incorporating Art into Life

Tadashi Kawamata (Japan/France)
169 *Matsunoyama Project*, 2000–ongoing | 170 *Matsunoyama Installation*, 2000
171 *Matsunoyama Project*, 2003 | 172 *Nakahara Yusuke Cosmology*, 2012

Perhaps there are aspects of the Echigo-Tsumari Art Triennale involving popular art and living art that may be uncomfortable to the sensibilities of fine-art purists. But Echigo-Tsumari deliberately aligns itself with an approach that serves the public and incorporates art into life. Tadashi Kawamata's work resonates with these lines of inquiry.

Kawamata has gained worldwide recognition for his careful consideration of how he lives as an artist. His involvement with the triennial since the first edition has helped Echigo-Tsumari attain a place on the international stage. During the first edition, he took the *hazaki* tree, which is used to dry rice in September, and created an installation out of it in July (*Matsunoyama Installation*). He also launched the *Matsunoyama Project,* a long-term workshop to create a plaza in the forest in collaboration with local residents and university students. He spent one month every year living in Matsunoyama, having dialogues with locals, before constructing the structure.

During the second triennial, Kawamata's *Matsunoyama Project* was part of the Echigo-Matsunoyama Museum of Natural Science, Kyororo, and involved the creation of hiking trails and an outdoor deck where people can enjoy the environment. He also erected thirty *mujin-ichi* structures (*mujin-hanbai-sho*, unmanned shops) throughout. He was interested in the idea of building a sense of goodwill and trust within the community by allowing for vegetables to be purchased using the honor system.

His idea for a third undertaking is a "live-in project," a permanent base wherein visitors can continue these activities, but this project is currently suspended. Perhaps because it would be deep in the mountains of Echigo-Tsumari, it may have been challenging for some to comprehend this approach as an artistic practice, despite my personal inclination in favor of his unique conceptual framework, not to mention the beauty of the site, the forest, and the surrounding environment. It may also have been a difficult situation for Kawamata because he was trying to relocate his studio to Paris at the time. It was a moment when he was broadening his expressive approach and gaining international recognition for his large-scale installations.

For the fourth triennial, Kawamata returned from France to Echigo-Tsumari to create a world archive for restorative urban/rural design practices through art, and we used the former Shimizu elementary school to establish the Inter-Local Art Network Center. Kawamata, who has been known to both criticize and promote the triennial internationally, planned to exhibit documents from art projects throughout the world and to organize open seminars, conferences, and forums with invited guests. I personally view this project as one of the successful models of transforming closed schools. It succeeds at being at the same time artwork, art institution, and archival art storehouse.

For the fifth triennial, the family of the late Yusuke Nakahara, who was an art critic and an advisor for the art festival, donated his collection of twenty thousand books, which Kawamata used for an installation called *The Cosmology of Yusuke Nakahara*. This exhibit was a success, and Kawamata stated, "Next to France, there is Echigo-Tsumari." His work has been crucial in archiving what the Echigo-Tsumari Art Triennale has accomplished thus far.

Questioning the Way of the Museum

173 Cai Guo-Qiang (China/USA), *Dragon Museum of Contemporary Art (DMOCA)*, 2000–ongoing

Is art better expressed in a neutral vacuum, or should it be aware of and specific to its site?

As visitors approach the steep, bouldered slope of Mountain Park Tsunan, they see a brick structure in the dense foliage. A side path leads to a panoramic view of the Shinano River and the spectacular, overlapping rice terraces. This is the site of Cai Guo-Qiang's Dragon Museum of Contemporary Art.

Cai is originally from Fujian Province in China. He brought with him a dragon kiln that was about to be demolished. The dragon kiln is a kind of Chinese climbing kiln that is built into a hillside to create an updraft inside. Unlike other kilns, it has no chambers; the interior is one continuous tube from the firebox to the chimney.

After the bricks and earth from the disassembled kiln and the pine used to harden it were delivered to Tsunan, four kiln experts and Cai's technical director, Masatoshi Tatsumi, and the Kohebi Volunteers got their hands dirty to rebuild it. For the opening in 2000, its spectacularly red flames could be seen from Tokamachi.

The Dragon Museum of Contemporary Art is both a functional dragon kiln and Cai's artwork. He is the director and curator of this museum. The many openings along the side of the kiln are used to view the pieces in it during the firing and to remove them after the firing. The kiln is a museum, and the openings are like entrances for guests.

A museum is only successful if there are people who want to see the artworks and artists who want to show their work. This fairly straightforward intent is often complicated by bureaucracy and money. Cai's museum is truly independent, since there is no outside curator, air-conditioning, insurance, or docents. The artist carries out all the duties of a director and curator by selecting the artists and organizing the production of the artwork. He has been directing the museum in this way every three years for all of the editions. I admire his sense of responsibility to this project, considering how busy he is as an internationally renowned artist, always flying around the world.

Kiki Smith produced a poetic piece for the museum called *Pause* in 2003, followed by Kotaro Miyanaga in 2006, Jennifer Wen Ma in 2009, and then Ann Hamilton in 2012.

On the face of the steep hill, the narrow exhibition space is dark and humid. It is unique in that it is an exhibition space inside of someone else's work. The space is riddled with constraints and parameters, but this is why the works thrive here. This distinct space challenges and counters the neutral white cube, producing a truly interesting phenomenon.

174 Kiki Smith (USA), *Pause*, 2003
   Pieces collaboratively built were housed inside the kiln.
   There were figurative sculptures of girls seated on stairs,
   bundles of firewood, cherry blossoms, and snowflakes,
   spinning a narrative within the forest.

175 Jennifer Wen Ma (China/USA),
   You Can't Always See Where You Are Going,
   But Can You See Where You've Been?, 2009
   The interior of the kiln museum was filled with
   nearly a ton of black sumi ink, which was like a black
   pond, reflecting visitors like a mirror. The walls
   of the kiln were painted with ink, contrasting green
   with pitch black.

176 | 177 | 178

176 Yoshiaki Ito (Japan),
   Tour de Tsumari, 2006–ongoing
177 Meschac Gaba (Benin / the Netherlands),
   The Game of Mikado, 2012
178 Yasuyuki Watanabe (Japan),
   Beat of the Ground, 2003–ongoing

Sounds to Open the Five Senses

Satoyama involves the relationship between nature and the entirety of human physiology. There are artists who respond physically in myriad ways to the sensuous qualities of *satoyama*, and who engage with sound as a way to express its allure.

For the first edition, Rolf Julius created a device to hear the sounds of the Matsudai Station underground passage from the remote mountain. Visitors could faintly hear the amplified sounds collected in the area coming from speakers, as well as the live sounds of birds, insects, and wind, making the silence more noticeable and guiding them.

Jonathan Bepler's *The Symphony of Hillocks: Oratorio for the Valley and Hills* (2003) was an audio CD for a drive through the *satoyama*. The "soundtrack on the move" was a symphony born of *satoyama*, locals, and visitors.

Henrik Håkansson's *The Waves of Sound* (2006, 2009) required participants to be seated with headphones listening to amplified sounds of the nature in front of them: plants swaying in the wind, birds, and insects.

Yasuyuki Watanabe's *Beat of the Ground* from 2003 is ongoing and involves making clay instruments with locals to perform sounds.

Physical Expression at Echigo-Tsumari

One of the unique events of the Echigo-Tsumari Art Triennale has been a tournament organized by Keita Kunitani called *Sports Hide-and-Seek*. The game was a combination of can kicking and hide-and-seek in three rounds, played by teams of participants wearing red and white, at a shrine, a schoolyard, and other locations. Visitors and locals play together, hiding in buildings and behind trees. The energy from running around is absorbed in the body, and the excitement is palpable in the air.

Performances with a strong sense of physicality have become increasingly significant. Video work at the triennial is somewhat limited, because visitors are traveling around to see works dispersed throughout the region, which is incompatible with video works that require sitting still indoors. Even among the performances, the events that are most successful tend to be those that require large dramatic movements, like *Tour de Tsumari* and *The Day After Tomorrow Football Tournament* (see page 231), which are athletic events. In 2012 *Mikado* games, which are popular in Europe, were played at life-size. Sports and games have a strong and compelling power that we plan to further engage.

180

Inaka: The Countryside as Site for Festive Performances

Performance is one aspect that I would like to further develop by having performance artists use empty houses and schools as stations for residency and production while engaging with the local people. I even like the idea of previewing performances before their official opening in Tokyo. Artists will develop a strong connection to the site, cultivating a link between the city and the country.

Today a performance company faces many challenges if it is to support itself solely through profits from its events. It is common for the artists to have part-time jobs to earn a living. Perhaps farming at Echigo-Tsumari while performing could be an interesting possibility.

One-time events require funding. Events that are in remote areas far from greater Tokyo require difficult work to gather an audience. Despite that, I like to organize them, because I think everyone needs time for celebratory rituals. One could receive support and funding from institutions, but that is not enough to cover the entire cost of production. A solution might be to raise funds primarily through the audience. In other words, the audience members become the patrons of the actors and management, and they determine the entertainment value of the work by choosing to pay or not. This follows the model of traditional Japanese performances and the history of the Noh artists Zeami and Kan'ami, who depended upon the support of audiences more than public funding and grants.

179 Beat Asia, 2009
This was a collaboration in music and dance between Ondekoza (a Japanese taiko drum group), Bimo Dance Theater and Kanahan (Indonesian dance and percussion groups), and Jinenjo Club (a group of people with special needs working on creative activities and organic farming).

180 Phare Ponleu Selpak (Cambodia), *Cambodian Circus Theater*, 2009, 2012
This was a contemporary circus performance incorporating theater, dance, and traditional performing arts.

181 World Drum Festival, 2006
World class drum masters L'ACOUSTEEL GANG (France), PURI (South Korea), Bami Jean Tsakeng (Cameroon), Hachijo Taiko, Bamboo Orchestra Japan, and Ondekoza performed, using the rice paddies as a stage.

182 Shigeya Mori (Japan), *Matsunoyama Genki Ekkenou Theater*, 2009
Shigeya Mori has continued to work on revitalizing communities in Echigo-Tsumari through traditional art performances since 2005.

183 Nibroll (Japan), *see/saw*, 2012
The title refers to vision. The performance was created and implemented in collaboration with local residents by incorporating their narratives, dances, and old tools. It was centered around the shrine.

184 Kanroku (Japan), *Matsudai Bunraku Gekijo*, 2006
Since 2003, Kanroku has been engaging the local residents to put on collaborative performances that go beyond conventional Bunraku performances.

Possibilities of Photography Explored in Echigo-Tsumari

The Echigo-Tsumari Art Triennale has included a number of photographic projects. During the first edition, a gigantic pinhole camera was created in a community of two hundred residents for Shin Egashira's field investigation titled *Slow Box + After Image.* The large-format pinhole camera recorded a slow-motion afterimage that was reflected onto a large glass sheet, representing time. The *Kamiebiike Museum of Art,* a project launched for the fourth triennial by Tetsuo Onari and Mikiko Takeuchi, was an exhibition of photographs of community people playing the characters of some of the world's most famous paintings. In 2006, a vacant house was altered into the *Myokayama Photo Gallery,* which captured portraits of visitors to be used at their funerals. In 2012, the *Asia Photography and Image Center* exhibited a compilation of contemporary photography of Asia. Photo documentation of the triennial has been carried out by the established photographers Shigeo Anzai (2000, 2003), Takenori Miyamoto (2006), Osamu Nakamura (2009), and Naoki Ishikawa (2012).

The first time I began to consider photography was during the second preevent in 2002, titled *An Offering to the Heavens,* when the ikebana (Japanese art of flower arrangement) artist Yukio Nakagawa released one million tulip petals from the sky above the Shinano riverbed. After a conversation with Daisuke Nakatsuka, who was the creative director for the poster and catalog for the second edition, we agreed that Nakagawa's ikebana performance would be shot by the photographer Daido Moriyama. Then Nakatsuka arranged for Moriyama to photograph Christian Bastiaans's *Real Lear* and edit a book called *Nirvana and Back,* featuring Moriyama's photographs of Echigo-Tsumari. Moriyama, who is known for black-and-white images of Shinjuku, produced brilliantly colorful photographs of flower gardens along the paths in Echigo-Tsumari. Bastiaans's reflection on Japanese society after high economic growth as being best represented in Echigo-Tsumari, rather than Tokyo, resonates with Moriyama through the photographs.

A photographer captures instinctual, physical phenomena. The immediacy of that act is appealing. Through the lens, one can directly connect a place to old memories and more broadly to the rest of the world. For the photographer and for the viewer, photography is light and is a means for building a narrative. For this reason, photography is an effective medium for Echigo-Tsumari.

When the fifth triennial ended, the Echigo-Tsumari Art Triennale and its artworks were in flux. Earlier many artists had used photography in their works, but recently we have been focused more on idea-based artists who contemplate time and place. Collecting artists from specific genres seemed to favor mediocrity, making it difficult for the best artists to shine. During the 2012 edition, the photographs of *mabu* (tunnels that were made to create rice fields) by Katsuhito Nakazato were a revelation that seemingly came from another world. Even the locals had not seen and did not know of *mabu,* and to capture them was to make an artwork with expressive means that was also a scientific geological investigation. This kind of work transcends the conventions of genre; it is interdisciplinary and multifaceted and challenges the viewer to ask, "Is this photography? Is this interesting?" The well-respected art critic Yusuke Nakahara, who passed away in 2011 and had been an advisor for the Echigo-Tsumari Art Triennale since its first edition, once described photography and video as "the fluctuation of embodiment of space-time manifestations that cross in succession, resulting in richness." Echigo-Tsumari must continue to be a dynamic and generative place as we reflect upon Nakahara's words at a time of increased homogeneity in modern time and space.

185 Daido Moriyama (Japan), *Nirvana and Back*, 2004
Daido Moriyama documented the performance
of *Real Lear* and photographed *satoyama* during
his visit. The work was published by the publisher
Gendaikikakushitsu.

——

186 *The Asia Photography and Image Center* (2012)
This exhibition of work by photographers from Japan
and China took place at the former Myokayama
Elementary School. The pavilion also included
Myokayama community documents in an archive and
on display. The photographs included *Tsumari Story*
by RongRong and inri.

187 Miya Nishio (Japan), *Familial Uniform*, 2009
Photographs from several decades ago were selected from
the three families that are part of the Iwase community.
The portraits were re-created using people wearing
the same clothes, at the same places. The photographs
were installed in their living spaces characterized by
terraced rice fields, houses, and alleys. This approach
redefines and captures the meaning of family and
intimacy in the community.

——

188 Katsuhito Nakazato (Japan),
Flash: Surface & Tunnel, 2012
The change of the course of the river to increase
terrain suitable for rice fields results in tunnels excavated
without timbering, which are called *mabu*. It is
estimated that hundreds of *mabu* have been created since
the end of the Edo period up through the Meiji and
Taishō periods.

188

Everything Made by Human Beings Is Art

Painting and sculpture in the West is generally regarded as autonomous—fine art as opposed to applied arts. Despite this designation, fine-art paintings cannot escape functionality. In Japan, paintings exist everywhere on *shoji* and *fusuma* doors and ceilings. In a sense, they are inseparable from furniture.

The cave paintings from Lascaux and Altamira are similar in this way. The prehistoric people hunted for food, ate the meat and dried the rest, saving the hide. When they had free time, they drew. Drawing was part of their lifestyle.

Dance is sometimes regarded as a pure form of art. But in the creation myths of Japan, there is the parable of Amaterasuoomikami, who hides in the deep *amanoiwato* cave as an angry retreat from the violence of Susanonomikoto. Amenouzume danced at the gate with her chest bared to lure him out, which made everyone laugh and dance. This is the origin of the first *matsuri*. *Matsuri* are not meant to be selective in terms of their participants, but rather something that is a part of life. A way of life here means you wake from sleep, have a meal, cultivate fields and rice paddies, fish and hunt, weave, and have children and raise them, and *matsuri* mark the passage of time within the daily routines. Nature, artifice, and the relationship between them is art. In other words, everything surrounding our lives can be considered art, or what I want to call "lifeway art."

The critic Shunsuke Tsurumi describes "pure art" as work made by specialists, accepted by institutions and experts in the field. He defines artwork created by specialists that is enjoyed by the general public as "popular arts." Artworks made by nonprofessionals that are widely accepted by the public he calls "marginal arts." *Yoitomake* songs, tongue twisters, and New Year's cards are part of daily life and they overlap with art; these are examples of what Tsurumi might call "marginal arts." This kind of categorization seems to stem from Western values. In my thinking, "lifeway art" suggests not only the art of survival but also ideological aspects. *Matsuri* and love letters are essential to the daily life struggle.

The desire and skill to engage with the local people around the natural environment that they contend with daily has become a central theme of the triennial. Simply put, how does one turn bamboo into a tool? This exemplifies quotidian life here and encapsulates the whole of art. *Ubusuna House,* the *Museum of Picture Book Art,* Yukihisa Isobe's *River Trilogy Project,* Mierle Landerman Ukeles's *Snow-Workers' Ballet,* and Christian Bastiaan's *Real Lear* were created with a thorough commitment to the region and the residents, and exemplify this kind of "lifeway art."

189 Yuko Nagumo (Japan), *Scrap and Bride*, 2009
A real-life couple was asked to wear an original bridal kimono from Tokamachi for the *hanayome-gyoretsu*, or wedding parade ritual. This imagery is a play on the old custom and adage of "throw away an old home to establish a new world." Four hundred family members, friends, locals, visitors to the festival, and staff participated in the parade extending from the Nagumo shrine to Yuinosato. The relics of the performance, such as the bride's kimono, were displayed at the former laboratory of an agricultural high school.

190 Takahide Mizuuchi (Japan), *Echigo—silent parade*, 2012
While moving slowly through four communities, floats sold vegetables or served drinks and became a salon of the village.

191 Satoshi Iwama (Japan), *Tsubono Field Park Satomatsuri*, 2012
For seventeen years, the artist has been working on revitalizing the traditional *minka* houses and terraced rice fields, coppicing the beech forests, and re-creating traditional storehouses in Tsubono village. For the *satomatsuri* festival the artist created a variety of events about food, bathing, and dance.

191

192

Food as Art

As part of the development of the triennial's future, I have plans to increase coordinators and mediators involved in the specialization of food. Food can easily be built into an artwork or event, and it enjoys a strongly favorable reception by the audience. It also serves as an important way for the locals to become the stars of Echigo-Tsumari.

At the 2009 and 2012 editions, *The Onigiri Rice Ball Circle* project lasted for several days and was extremely popular. The settlement becomes a stage at high noon when one hears the words, "Would you like a rice ball?" Those calling are mothers from the settlement and Kohebi Volunteers. Banners that signify rice balls are raised and the freshly made rice balls and pickles are unveiled. The staging of the event varies depending on the community; some even have elaborate flower decorations added to the outer wrappings. The invited guests greet each other and sit in a circle, speak with local residents, and enjoy a rice ball. Echigo-Tsumari is known for the production of Uonuma Koshihikari brand rice, which is daily rice for the locals but special for the visitors.

After the food is consumed, the guests express gratitude in response to the invitation, which completes this performative work. Gratitude is expressed in whatever way one wishes. Some prepare a special gift, while others sing or bring instruments. Some even perform magic. In just a brief time, people who did not know one another connect through rice balls. The traveler from the outside graciously responds to the hospitality of the locals. The memorable time shared between host and guest is fleeting but significant.

In 2012, Rirkrit Tiravanija performed *Curry nō Curry.* Thai cuisine has been essential to Tiravanija's works for many years. He used fresh vegetables and pork from Tsumari and shared the curry with visitors to engage them in communication. Even before this there were food-related works, such as *The Berry Spoon*, wherein berries are grown and cultivated, and people are engaged through the context of food and art.

Sometimes visitors utter the question, "How is this an art piece?" but it always has a lasting impression. This kind of work is uncommon at other art festivals and I intend to continue fostering it in the future.

And how is it different from other restaurants or food services? It's not the formal composition of the food in the artwork, but rather the entire context of the food that is the art. Take *The Onigiri Rice Ball Circle*, which was conceived by Kohebi Volunteers to connect visitors with the community even without an artist or artwork being involved. This undertaking required many meetings and the cooperation of the various communities, and the local women enthusiastically volunteered to participate.

We have likewise channeled our energy into examples outside of the art projects, such as the menu from the *Ubusuna House*, NOHBUTAI, and the *East Asia Art Village*. They subscribe to the notion of food as the foundation of culture and art. In a poor mountain community, it would not make sense to serve visitors whatever they ordinarily like to eat at home. Instead, local food that is fresh and seasonal is strongly emphasized in the menus, and while eating, one senses the hands and efforts of the local chef and service staff. There are various directors, artists, and locals who all partake in building these menus. It is our mission to create unforgettable foods that can only be tasted here, at this place.

—

192 *The Onigiri Rice Ball Circle,* 2009, 2012
Everyone sits together in a circle under red flags, and local residents serve rice balls and pickles to guests. Guests express gratitude in some way after eating.

—

193 To the woods (Japan/Austria),
Berry Spoon, 2003–ongoing
This art project involved growing berries to form community. More than thirty kinds of berries were planted in the field. The colors of the plants change depending on the season. The locals can be observed patiently weeding. The idea of farming as art connects people with the joys of life.

194 Meal in Kamakura
(program of the Lunar New Year tour)

—

195 Rirkrit Tiravanija (Thailand/Argentina/USA),
Curry nô Curry, 2012
Curry was prepared for participants, and communities engaged in conversation. The Thai pork curry was made from ingredients found in Echigo-Tsumari, and another curry recipe was created by the locals.

Ikebana

196 Yukio Nakagawa (Japan), *An Offering to Heaven: Hanagurui,* 2002

The ikebana artist Yukio Nakagawa dropped one million tulip petals from the sky on May 18, 2002. This piece was performed as the preevent of the second triennial. Shortly before it was to take place, we discovered that many of the prepared petals had mold growing on them. Phone calls were made all over Japan to collect another one hundred thousand petals. Finally, on the day of the performance at 1 PM, the petals began to drop from a helicopter. Beneath the dancing petals, the ninety-five-year-old *butoh* dancer Kazuo Ohno waved his hand as if to celebrate this choreographed, massively colorful moment. For the four thousand people who gathered to watch, these few minutes were an unforgettable experience.

Feeling the life force, the sense of the sublime, in Nakagawa's ikebana performance was amazing, but I also appreciate the simple practice of displaying a flower in one's *tokonoma* (reception room) as part of Japanese daily life. This is the connection to the gardens along paths in Echigo-Tsumari. We placed a new emphasis on ceramics and ikebana following the third triennial. The *akiya* in the Koshirakura settlement during the third, and the Yomogihira settlement in the fourth and fifth editions, became backdrops for works by ikebana artists beyond the different styles of ikebana schools. Many of the artists were well established and elderly yet have tremendous energy and vitality. I yearn for younger artists to show this kind of vitality in their work. Contemporary approaches to ikebana seem to superficially mimic modern art movements and are unable to break free from the rules and conventions of the medium of flower arrangement. Perhaps artists and architects must also recognize the banality of adopting a medium and its materiality as the sole formal agenda for a work.

One of my interests is community gardening. Since 2009, Yutaka Kawaguchi and Kaori Naito have created gardens of indigenous plants along paths that connect the houses of the Hoshitoge settlement. This approach seems to be a natural way of incorporating flowers and plants into the community and fits Echigo-Tsumari.

197 Takatoshi Shimoda (Japan), *Dwelling of Wind,* 2009

198 Yuichiro Hinata (Japan),
What Makes Plants Speak, 2006
The Group F, consisting of ikebana artists of different schools, including Yuichiro Hinata, sought to create new ikebana approaches. They created arrangements in the Koshirakura settlement in 2006, and in the Yomogihira settlement *akiya* in 2009.

199 Yutaka Kawaguchi and Kaori Naito (Japan),
The Place Where a Garden Is Born, 2009–ongoing
The artists created gardens of indigenous plants as a practice that harkens back to the starting point of *satoyama,* the nature and human interface. The gardens continuously grow and change.

Asian Networking Platform: The East Asia Art Village

In midwinter of 2004, we began a contest at the theater of the Matsudai Snow-Land Agrarian Culture Center NOHBUTAI called the Echigo-Tsumari version of the Kohaku Singing Contest, a national contest that is widely televised on New Year's Eve. The participants are primarily locals, and I noticed that some of the singers were the Chinese, Korean, and Filipina wives of locals, who had immigrated to Echigo-Tsumari. They sang songs of *enka* singers such as Misora Hibari. They listen to such songs every night. I would guess that they spend their days feeling isolated and weeping silently in a foreign country where the language is difficult and assimilation is challenging. I was moved by their voices as if resonating with a blizzard. It was a definitive experience for me.

When I researched the number of immigrant wives who came to Echigo-Tsumari from Southeast and Northeast Asia, I found that Tsunan Town had the largest population of them. This is one way in which the demographics of these rural communities suffering depopulation have connected with the world outside of Japan.

The East Asia Art Village was first conceived with the establishment of the Dragon Museum of Contemporary Art. Over ten years since then, collaborations with the residents have expanded to the Uwano, Anayama, and Ashidaki communities.

One of the participants was Korean artist Kim Koohan, who lived in the Uwano settlement for a period of one year to construct a clay house, which was fired to become the *House of Magpies* and

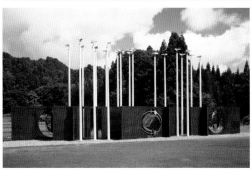

became part of a park. This was the result of cultural exchanges that were difficult at first. Prejudices had to be overcome. Shinichi Ikehata said at the report meeting of the second triennial: "Please note that this is not racial prejudice, but when Mr. Kim came to Uwano, he did not do anything except go to the *onsen* bath and drink sake. We wondered how we should treat him. But he started working seriously, and then the residents changed their attitude toward him. We brought him gifts and helped him. He made efforts to complete the work. As a result, we had less prejudice toward Koreans and even want to start an Uwano brand ceramic industry with him in our community."

Beginning with the Uwano settlement, we want to find ways to foster Koreans and other immigrants and people from overseas. We also want this to be a place where people from Asia and beyond can casually and easily visit on holidays.

In 2009, the Uwano Community Center was refurbished into residences for artists and gallery spaces. Works were created by the Hong Kong artist Kingsley Ng in the Ashidaki settlement, the Taiwanese artist Lin Shuen Long in the Anayama settlement, and the Chinese artist Guan Huaibin in the Uwano settlement. In May 2010, through these cultural interactions, the community of Anayama became a sister village to two villages in Taiwan. In 2012, the Uwano Community Center was turned into the East Asia Art Center, for which Sense Art Studio from Hong Kong played a role as director. The exchange among these Asian regions is an essential part of community building in this region.

This movement began in 2013 during the second Setouchi Triennale, unveiled in the form of the Fukutake House Asian Art Platform, an effort to establish a sustainable network concerning art and culture foundations and institutions of seven Asian countries and regions. This network will carry over to Echigo-Tsumari.

For the sixth triennial, junior high and high school students from Hong Kong will be part of the Kohebi Volunteer troops. Former members of the Hong Kong Kohebi Volunteers were concerned about the low food self-sufficiency of Hong Kong and decided to send young people to learn about agriculture from Echigo-Tsumari so that they can apply it to their own contexts and visions.

—

200 Koohan Kim (South Korea), *House of Magpies*,
2003–ongoing
Clay, sand, fire, and wood are essential materials used in this house. The artist incorporated inlay techniques to create imagery inspired by the region and the story that all creations return to the earth.

Kohebi Volunteers from Hong Kong and Shanghai

201 Lin Shuen Long (Taiwan),
Beyond Borders, 2009–ongoing
The artist made a gate using traditional Taiwanese craft techniques. There is a bronze of a water buffalo, which symbolizes Taiwan's agriculture, in a park where the cultures of Taiwan and the community are interconnected.

—

202 Guan Huaibin (China),
The Voyage Beyond Time, 2009–ongoing
This work is installed in a gateball park at Uwano, where round mirrors reflect the surroundings.

—

203 Jae-Hyo Lee (South Korea), *0121-1110=109071*,
2009–ongoing
Three spheres made out of wood are installed in the Mountain Park Tsunan. The works are intended to be covered by vegetation, becoming part of the environment.

204

205

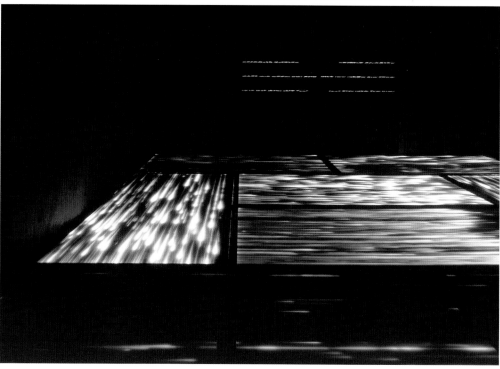

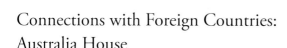

211

Connections with Foreign Countries:
Australia House

The Australia House represents the strong relationship we have had with Australia since the first triennial. Australia shares some geopolitical conditions with Japan. Japan is an archipelago and Australia is a continent, both floating in the Pacific Ocean, sandwiched by the superpower of the United States and the large populations of Asia. We know that the Australian government has recognized and attempted to pay homage to important indigenous peoples who immigrated to the continent forty thousand years ago.

For the first triennial, the artist Fiona Foley, who is of aboriginal descent, created the work *Dharma Eye.* Anne Graham started a food program and organized a party called Australia Night with the Australian embassy, which featured Aussie beef and wine, and more than one hundred guests were invited. The Australian didgeridoo was played, and the members of the embassy seemed to fully enjoy the party. Every organization has some staff members who can be engaged in nation-to-nation relationships with respect to indigenous or minority cultures. Through this event, our relationship with Australia developed and moved on to the next phase, through shared experience.

For the second triennial, three Australian artists were committed to the *akiya* projects in Uwayu community of Matsunoyama, where Marina Abramović's *Dream House* is located. The Mayer

257

aboriginal art collection, ordinarily housed at the Australian Melbourne Museum, was exhibited to commemorate the opening of the Museum of Natural Science Kyororo. The Mayer people, the director of the Melbourne Museum, and members of the embassy attended the opening and gave three-day tours.

For the third triennial, an Australian curator stayed in Echigo-Tsumari for three months to assist in the festival. The Australia House was established as a residence and gallery using a vacant house at the Toyoda community of forty people in Urada, a remote mountainous settlement in the Matsunoyama area, although it was destroyed in the earthquake on March 12, 2011. Subsequently, we organized an international design competition chaired by Tadao Ando for the new Australia House. The parameters of the new design were that it needed to be economical, compact, and hazard-resistant. The design selected from the 154 proposals was by Andrew Burns Architects. The triangular sculptural design utilizes cedar planks that blend well into the surroundings. This design won the Jørn Utzon Award for International Architecture, an award by the designer of the Sydney Opera House, given here for the first time to a design in Japan.

International exchange can take a number of forms. Eventually, it may be imaginable for the people of the region of Urada to travel to an aboriginal community. The world can be connected through small communities. This human-scale network that envelops the world makes for amazing possibilities.

204 Fiona Foley (Australia), *Dharma Eye,* 2000
Two golden boats floated in a pond with eleven hundred boards cut into the shapes of leaves. The leaves clearly referenced botanical specimens of the region.

205 Janet Laurence (Australia), *Elixir,* 2003–ongoing
A traditional wooden storehouse has been refurbished into a bar, allowing for visitors to drink distilled spirits infused with local plants. Glass panels house sketches and texts related to local herbal studies and medicine.

206 Lauren Berkowitz (Australia), *Harvest House,* 2003–ongoing
The artist transformed the traditional *minka* into a space consisting of textile, harvest, landscape, and charcoal rooms that evoke the history and memory of the transformed space.

207 Robyn Backen (Australia), *Rice Talk,* 2003–ongoing
Optical fibers are embedded into the tatami mats on the second floor of the *Harvest House* and spell out a haiku by Kobayashi Issa in Morse code. Text is also spelled out in the windows.

208 Australia House, 2009–11

209 Andrew Burns Architects (Australia), *Australia House,* 2012–ongoing

210 Brook Andrew (Australia), *Dhirrayn ngurang—Mountain Home,* 2012–ongoing
The artist, who is of aboriginal descent, wrote a poem based on interviews with residents, which is written with neon lights onto aboriginal traditional patterns on a wall that serves as a hidden door of the gallery.

211 Anne Graham (UK/Australia), *Snake Path,* 2003–ongoing
The snaking path along the former Nakasato community campsite extends for 140 meters. More than four hundred people of more than seventy groups, including Newcastle University students, participated in and completed the project.

Essay

The Art of Tourism in Rural Japan:
Footnotes of an Itinerant Architect

Lynne Breslin

Since the Meiji Restoration, the Japanese have increasingly exercised their right to travel both at home and abroad.[1] Within Japan, tourism has itself become an art form, introducing (first) Japanese and (later) foreigners to the geographically—and often psychologically and historically—distant remote. The richness of the experience has been carefully honed, with its lineage of practices, ranging from novels to guides, cultural and commercial exhibitions, nostalgic re-creations, and cultural pilgrimages, responding to internal and external influences.

Since 1978, I have traveled to Japan frequently. Recently, I have been drawn in particular to Echigo-Tsumari and the Seto Islands because of their profound reservoirs of art, natural beauty, and authentic communities. These two revolutionary art experiences in rural Japan, one on a group of islands and the other in the Japanese Alps, present physical and mental odysseys. I find myself lost, far from familiar urban landscapes. The extensive national public transportation system dead-ends before the eroding villages, half-fallow fields, and forested mountains, which have been interrupted by astounding artistic incursions. These art programs take me to places I've never been before; they are a gateway to emerging and challenged expressions of community and cultural potential. On my many visits, I have had time to reflect on how to penetrate this hidden, repressed Japan. These are my footnotes on the context of these rural art festivals.

Murakami, Trains, and Borders

From afar, the novelist Haruki Murakami has guided me through a Japan riddled with unresolved political and social traumas. Before Murakami, Yasunari Kawabata's *Snow Country* (1935–37) and Yukio Mishima's *Sound of Waves* (1954) were my first introductions to the wetlands of the mountain region (*satoyama*) and sea islands and coastal regions (*satoumi*). Murakami, however, opened the door to a more layered Japan, exposing the underbelly of the supercool, revealing the shadows of authoritarianism. Murakami reckons with the evils of cults, politicians with ties to World War II, and the cruel actions of one's peers. Bullying, a common theme, reflects a chain reaction of social relations from childhood to adult soldiers, mired in moral collusion.

Tsukuru Tazaki, the hero of his recent novel *Colorless Tsukuru Tazaki and His Years of Pilgrimage* (2014), is a railroad station engineer and the victim of bullying. His escape is watching trains depart for distant towns; he himself never boards. At the end of the story, this pilgrim of consciousness contemplates the wonder of a trip on an express train to Matsumoto, a remote castle town in the mountains. Tazaki is finally able to put his past into perspective after traveling. For the novelist, travel is that road to self-knowledge: "the rear light of consciousness, like the last express train of the night." Only separation from the everyday and every place can produce this awareness and lead to true understanding. Tourism has been described as the practice of immaterial, intangible, sensual, and psychological experiences, requiring physical displacement.[2] Several of Murakami's heroes find the Tokyo train station, Shinjuku, the beginning of the path to existential clarity and an alternative hyperreality, leading to greater understanding.[3]

Hiroshige and the Bridge from East to West

In Japan, illustrated guides and virtual tours have always been popular, a sign of the importance of travel for work and pleasure and the desire to see beyond. Many early guides registered the best-known sights in the Kansai region of Kyoto, Osaka, and Nara, and facilitated travel to and from Edo (as Tokyo was known before 1868). These texts mapped social relations in addition to material artifacts. Hiroshige Utagawa's *53 Stations of the Tokaido* (1834), a series of fifty-five woodblock prints, was a groundbreaking kind of travel guide. A radical appropriation of landscape, the prints internalized Western perspective but came to represent the ideal of the Japanese picturesque for the rest of the world. Vincent van Gogh paraphrased moments of these landscape storyboards, and Frank Lloyd Wright declared them "some of the most valuable contributions ever made to the art of the world."[4] This printed tour of mid-nineteenth-century Japan from Edo to Kyoto set the stage for framing scenery and its carefully orchestrated consumption by the tourist and the would-be tourist. A distilled journey from site to site, it offered a way of curating large regions and prescribing experiences. It offered a mandate for comprehending a distant landscape: a catalog of worthy places and times (seasons) to be appreciated.

Hiroshige Utagawa's *53 Stations of the Tokaido* (1834). Hiroshige depicts workers in perspective.

Other prints and guides had mapped the features of the city, for instance, *Pictures of Famous Places of Edo*, begun by Yukio Saito (1737–1799) and illustrated by Hasegawa Settan. Hiroshige followed his *53 Stations* and *View of 60 Odd Provinces* (1856) with *100 Famous Views of Edo* (1858). His focus was increasingly shifting to the emerging city and its developing urban culture, a by-product of the Meiji development. Kiyochika Kobayashi, in his *Famous Views of Tokyo* (1876–81) and later the *100 Views of New Tokyo* (1928–32, featuring eight printmakers), continued to celebrate the city and catalog its increasing number of Western innovations.

The inroads of modernity accelerated, eclipsing tradition and the topography of a more traditional, rural Japan. The earlier depictions of mountains, bridges, and cloud formations were supplanted by these tokens of the new civilization: miniature golf courses, subways, department stores, cafes. The countryside remained but was subsumed by the new imported public enterprises. The Japanese flaneurs observed the modern stamp on everyday life. *Bunmei Kaika* (Civilization and Enlightenment), the crash course in modernity that was launched by the Meiji emperor, occurred almost entirely in the city. This colonizing of space and spirit gradually displaced the rural past and traditions. The guides once needed to navigate the wonders of the distant landscape were now tools to interpret the mystery of new city sites. In Japan, Tokyo became the other: the Westernized, transformed new metropolis. The divide between East and West was internalized as urban versus rural.[5] As the twentieth century progressed, the hinterlands became a distant past, increasingly removed from tourists' horizons.

Searching for the Authentic Outside of Tokyo: Following the Pilgrims and Matsuri

As early as the ninth century, the pilgrimage—wandering through unfamiliar landscapes—became a popular means of expressing Buddhist commitment. This tradition prescribed routes and practices that offered ordinary people a means of spiritual pursuit. Meanwhile, the ritual sustained marginal economies in these remote areas. This practice persists today.

As of the eighth century, on the scenic island of Shikoku, eighty-eight (Buddhist) temples and (Shinto) shrines were scattered over a mountainous 750-mile coarse terrain. Historically, pilgrims devoted one to two months to the journey, attired in special Henro costumes and cone-shaped hats, carrying walking sticks and a book that recorded the stamp of each temple station. Gradually, more than two hundred additional temples and shrines were added to the route, allowing these followers of the teachings of Kukai, a monk and founder of Shigon Buddhism also known as Kobo Daishi, to offer coins and prayers and enjoy the spectacular landscape. Not incidentally, the pilgrims became an increasingly important source of revenue for the poor temples and surrounding villages. The landscape, known for its spiritual power, retained its attraction over the centuries and accommodated the growing commercial concerns. Tourists joined the elderly pilgrims in exploring the past. Other pilgrim routes were developed in other areas of the country, replicating this successful model. Local *matsuri* also generated income for communities and provided links to distant traditions and activities. Tourists traveled to remote areas to participate in the celebrations.[6] The festivals varied by region, season, and content. Most villages or neighborhoods produced *matsuri* with distinctive, specific features and forms— a unique way of honoring or appeasing their resident *kami* (spirits, relating to the indigenous Shinto religion).

Sado Island, May 2005. Local *matsuri* with music, costumes, and food. Photo by author.

Many of the *matsuri* were cultivated for hundreds of years and were instrumental in fostering local identity. Often linked to natural phenomena and repeated annually, these elaborate celebrations occupied residents throughout the year and attracted visitors from the outside as well as locals. They involved special foods, dances, costumes, activities, and often parades of intricately decorated floats, some of them preserved for centuries. A special storehouse for the floats and costumes can still be found in most villages. A special economy developed around these yearly celebrations and the accommodation of visitors. Following the dense schedule of *matsuri* was a cherished means of participating in the age-old rhythms of everyday life in old Japan.

Arata Isozaki and His Return to the Past: A Postmodern Voyage

In his 2006 book *Japan-ness in Architecture,* Arata Isozaki, the noted architect, calls the *palanquin* (floats) of the *matsuri* and the stations of the pilgrimage an "architecture of events."[7] Japanese architecture, he says, differs from Western architecture in its performative quality, its dynamic characteristics. Whereas Western architecture is static and revels in its stasis, traditional Japanese building is in constant flux and often only the columns and roof remain unchangeable. The walls are easily rearranged or removed, transforming the functions of rooms and the overall appearance. The layers to the outside are easily modified, adjusting views and exposures according to function, time of day, or season.

Japan's most important national shrine, the Ise Shrine, has been disassembled and rebuilt on alternating sites every twenty years since 692 CE. The architecture is itself deceptively simple and hidden from view, obscured by a series of fences. The significance of the building lies in both the symbolic and the actual activity of the community, as it convenes to (re)build; the community itself is re-created every twenty years as it assembles for the event. It is the *act* of building rather than the physical construction that is critical.

Isozaki's influence cannot be overstated. Since the 1970s, he has been a leading thinker and theorist of Japanese architecture and culture. A protégé of Kenzō Tange, he has persistently questioned the nature of a public national architecture and forged his own response to modernism. Just recently, an exhibition at the Watari Museum of Contemporary Art in Tokyo reconstructed his private tree house and examined, once again, his incredible contribution to modern architectural theory.

In 1978, Isozaki inaugurated the traveling exhibition *Ma: Space-Time in Japan*.[8] Opening first in Paris, it presented an inspired interpretation of Japanese aesthetics to a foreign audience. It also became a formal opportunity for Isozaki to further explore his relationship to Japanese architectural tradition.[9] The goal was to examine the principles of *ma* and the potential of Japanese traditional aesthetics in a modern context. Almost impossible to explain, *ma* represents the coincidental conceptualization of time and space. Einstein's theory of relativity developed the notion of the interrelationship of time and space, but that twentieth-century theory is a complicated mathematical paradigm, while the Japanese theory of *ma* is ancient and intuitive, and extends to every aspect of Japanese life. Isozaki's interpretation of the space/time phenomena of *ma* is fully developed in his later descriptions of the performative nature of architecture, as in *Japan-ness in Architecture*.

The overlapping of time and space gives Japanese architecture, gardens, and practices, such as the *matsuri*, their unusual character. Perspectival space (celebrated as the great invention of the Italian Renaissance) is a construct that had been explored in Japanese art but largely rejected because it fails to describe the Japanese concept of space. Space is understood as frames of two dimensions negotiated through time. The flatness of space can be observed in the traditional arts, but also for instance in the absence of depth of field in Yasujiro Ozu's films, which have been noted as cinematographic translations of traditional Japanese space concepts.[10]

Isozaki and the Exhibition Rethought

Ma: Space-Time in Japan also represented a new type of exhibition, with its conceptually thematic, linked, newly commissioned works of art that elaborated and expanded on the theme. The artworks were secondary to the development of ideas. While still contained in a gallery, the exhibition "borrowed space," looking to extend the field of vision.[11] In one section, titled *michiyuki* (literally "travel" or "journey"), Isozaki commissioned Issey Miyake, the fashion designer, to create dressed mannequins, which were poised around an abstracted Noh stage. The "actors" appeared to move from the spirit world/past to the stage/present while dressed in *michiyukis* (traveling overcoats). Both the form—the staging and content—and the subject matter constructed a model of the space-time continuum.

As the commissioner of Artpolis, which launched in Kumamoto in 1988, Isozaki finally took an exhibition outdoors, beyond the confines of the museum, to explore the role of architecture as a catalyst for community. He drew upon his experience as a participant in the IBA: International Building Exhibition Berlin. This urban renewal project, which lasted from 1979 to 1987, commemorated the 750th anniversary of the founding of Berlin and enlisted international celebrity architects to design a variety of buildings that were strategically sited to stimulate both redevelopment and tourism. Amplifying this formula, Isozaki was able to interest the governor of Kumamoto Prefecture, Morihiro Hosokawa (later the prime minister of Japan), to launch a program of urban planning and architecture throughout the region. Both public and private buildings, civil engineering projects, and infrastructure commissions, were given to Japanese and international architects and engineers. Many of the commissions went to young and relatively unknown Japanese architects.

More than eighty projects were eventually completed for this contemporary comprehensive festival/exhibition, including housing, museums, police stations, sewage plants, tunnel ventilation projects, and public toilets, among others. The projects were distributed throughout the prefecture, some in remote villages. Like with the projects in Echigo-Tsumari and the Seto Islands, movement between the sites was difficult and required public and private transportation. Kumamoto is located in the east of Kyushu Island and, like so many rural regions of Japan, it was experiencing population loss and a decline of agriculture that threatened economic and social stability. The stated objective of Artpolis was that each project would aim to revitalize local cultures (and, thus, economic stability) by highlighting the unique characteristics of the region.

The name chosen, Artpolis, was intentional. From the start it engendered art production and social responsibility. Isozaki described his ambition as the creation of a "social structure" that would bring modernism, progress, and economic aid to a remote region of the country.[12] The commissioned projects created a network of points, and while there was no physical master plan, there was an overriding directive to create installations that would attract critical attention and outside visitors; the common thread was a connection to nature and the past, and artistic interest that would stimulate tourism.

Representative of the more successful private/public projects, the Seiwa Bunraku Puppet Theater designed by Kazuhiro Ishii now attracts more than one hundred thousand visitors per year. The novel architecture involves a sophisticated contemporary adaption of traditional all-wood construction techniques. The complex, consisting of a theater, exhibition space, and conference/cafe space, is a virtuoso exercise in elaborate wood joinery that depended on both the computer and the carpenter to come to fruition; traditional craft met technology with astounding results. The enclave, which now hosts seventeenth-century theater performances, has enabled a remote village of 3,800 people to persist.

Other projects, such as the Tamana City Observatory, draw attention to the incredible physical beauty of the region and include earth, cloud, and star chambers. Like so many of the projects, the City Observatory houses a community facility. This shared utopian ambition to use art to reengineer community is evident in almost every one of these projects. In the past twenty-five years, architects, students, and tourists have made their way to remote Kumamoto to visit this extensive exhibition of architecture. The program has since inspired at least four more Artpolis initiatives, in Okayama, Toyama, Shiroishi, and Hiroshima, each with the ambition of stimulating economic growth, improved quality of life, and tourism.[13]

Tourism as a National Priority and the Production of the Local

Following a government policy in the 1970s and early 1980s, the "production of locality" encouraged greater geographical differentiation and fostered local culture projects as a way to stimulate tourism outside the major cities of Tokyo and Kyoto. Festivals, theme parks, and villages (*furusatos*) were developed to attract domestic tourism and provide needed income to failing communities. Migration to cities since the Meiji era, and especially after World War II, had reduced the working population in many rural areas. And as urban concentration grew exponentially, the economic basis of the outlying areas was undermined by agricultural subsidy policies. In 1984, the LDP (the ruling party for most of the postwar years) introduced its Proposal for Furusato Japan to stimulate "culture" and resuscitate areas in distress. The Furusato Information Center in 1985, under the direction of the Ministry of Agriculture, Forests, and Fisheries, was directed to develop a tourist network. The national railroads promoted these native culture centers.

Satoyama *and* Satoumi

The economic decline of outlying mountainous and coastal areas increasingly threatened the ecology of Japan. And the Ministry of Environment, in identifying the risks to the ecosystems of the *satoyama* and *satoumi*, warned that human well-being was in jeopardy as well.[14] This issue of national importance directly related to what has consistently been identified as a uniquely Japanese symbiotic relationship between society and nature. The harmonic life, nurtured for centuries in outlying areas, depended on the careful management of natural resources in harsh and fabulously beautiful landscapes. Now overgrown, reconfigured, or host to invasive alien species (such as in golf courses), these *satoyama* regions were no longer supporting rice fields and lumber industry as in the past. Post-growth economic policies had undermined a careful balance maintained for centuries. This was also true of the coastal areas. The *satoumi* once sustained salt distilling as well as fishing and hemp bleaching, traditional means of employment that were becoming increasingly outsourced or obsolete. Now the government was encouraging ecotourism and the corresponding development of local institutions to attract tourists as a last-ditch effort to reverse the abandonment and natural decay of these areas.

Preservation and Jennifer Robinson

The preservation movement began in earnest in the late 1980s and was instrumental in identifying specific histories and practices associated with these differentiated regions. Private companies as well as local and national government agencies created *furusato, zukuri,* and *muras*: themed collections of buildings that were transported and reconstructed to create outdoor museums and simulate authentic villages of the past. Kaitaku-no Mura, outside of Sapporo, is a 119-acre open-air museum with a collection of early Hokkaido buildings from the Meiji period. Demonstrations of community bring the buildings to life. Museum staff and volunteers dress up and reenact boat making and craft production; however, the theme-park context frustrates a more nuanced reading of the city and the colonization of the indigenous local population of Ainus. A traditional wood-style fishing house from the nineteenth century, for instance, faces a three-story newspaper office building with a cast-iron facade.[15]

The Hida Folk Village (Hida no Sato), outside of Takayama in the mountains, brings together *gassho* farmhouses and exhibitions of farming practices and handicrafts. Children are invited to participate in archery and craft making. It also epitomizes these projects, which are part museum and part theme park, and more entertaining than authentic. Strict adherence to museum conventions is missing. Documentation is often uneven. And every opportunity is taken to monetize. The restaurants and souvenir shops are highly developed.

The number of these villages has multiplied in the last thirty years. The Meiji Mura, one of the earliest ones, outside of Nagoya (and a must-see for architects, since it contains the foyer of the Frank Lloyd Wright Imperial Hotel), can be toured by a miniature railway. Each stop on the tour provides a stamp with a lined drawing that visitors take away. These souvenirs are part of the ritual of visiting, mimicking the stamps pilgrims once collected.

In her essay "It Takes a Village: Internationalization and Nostalgia in Postwar Japan," Jennifer Robinson describes what she calls "double nostalgia." The creation

Hida no Sato. Scenes from the folk village outside of Takayama.
Houses were brought to the site to accommodate visitors.
The *gassho* houses were assembled from several nearby villages. Photo by
participants of the Columbia University GSAPP Art Space Workshop, 2014.

of *furusato*, she says, suggests a "generalized nature of such places." The tourist-destination *furusato* projects a desired vision of rustic artlessness in verdant landscapes. The "pastness, historicity, age, quaintness—[the] patina of familiarity and naturalness" are important. "Reconstructed or reinvented under the auspices of *furusato-zukuri* programs, these artifacts and practices, such as thatched-roof farmhouses and festivals (*matsuri*), can always only approximate actual historical forms, while the lifestyle associated with them is reified as timelessly and authentically 'Japanese.' Native place-making programs thus facilitate loss even as they compensate for the ontological anxiety of loss."[16]

Disasters and New Opportunities for Tourism

Jordan Sands in *Tokyo Vernacular* (2013) points out the underlying fusion of culture and economics in identifying tourist destinations and the success of the tourist industry in Japan.[17] The development of remote art festivals is a result of both government policies and regional political support of these cultural formations. The ventures are not limited to the countryside. In recent years, the Japanese government has utilized art in responding to several instances of urban decline. In Kobe, the Happy Active Town was instituted after the 1995 Great Hanshin earthquake. Tadao Ando's vast and empty Hyogo Art Museum and the Earthquake Memorial Museum, part of the Disaster Reduction and Human Renovation Institution, anchor this newly developed section of Kobe, which became home for one hundred thousand people displaced by the earthquake. Providing an active and meaningful life for the elderly was one clearly stated objective of the planning.

Faced with entrenched economic decline in areas of Yokohama, the city government supported the 2009 BankART project because "art generates urban renewal." The mayor, Hiroshi Nakada, stated that he wanted to celebrate Yokohama's cultural legacy, on the occasion of the port's 150-year anniversary, by attracting film industries and art. The goal was to transform the red-light district into artist housing and initiate Creative City Yokohama. Both BankART and the Yokohama Art Triennial were crucial to this initiative, which in turn owed much to the 2010 book *Creative Cities: A Toolkit for Urban Innovators* by Charles Landry. The organizers cited Landry's strategy of creativity (by government agencies) and the tactical contribution of the arts for urban renewal. Two far more nuanced and critical books by Sharon Zukin— *Loft Living* (1982) and *The Culture of Cities* (1995)—describe the role of artists in (first) stimulating the housing market and (then) producing images, memories, and the stuff of cultural consumption. Artists, Zukin argues, help frame a vision and propel "the city's symbolic economy."[18] This attracts tourists and capital and leads to redevelopment.

The Echigo-Tsumari and Setouchi Seto Island Triennials: Rediscovery of Culture

Raymond Williams uses the word "culture" to signify a whole way of life, including organizing means of production and creating arts and learning.[19] "Cultivation" includes growing crops, but also making art. In Echigo-Tsumari, standing on the viewing platform of the Matsudai Snow-Land Agrarian Culture Center NOHBUTAI, designed by the Netherlands-based architectural firm MVRDV, art and agriculture converge. The building resembles a hovering alien spaceship. It houses a retro classroom (absent a teacher) that unfolds, its drawers opening to exhibit a fabulous collection of natural artifacts. Outside, terraced rice paddies are freshly planted and are host to yellow metal silhouettes of laborers wearing traditional straw hats.[20] Texts in the foreground narrate the saga of farming the fields against a backdrop of mountains. This seemingly pop piece by Ilya and Emilia Kabakov (2000) is a real departure from the artists' usual reconstructions of Soviet realist mise-en-scènes and discourses on totalitarian society.

Both Western and Asian artists have found the space and time to reconsider content and form here in Echigo-Tsumari. Growing rice and adopting abandoned paddies are approached as creative acts. The creative process becomes richer and more complicated as cast and audience constantly exchange places, improvising and discovering new significances. When I first experienced the triennial, I did not expect to be focused so closely on the beauty of the rice fields—to follow the processing of rice and the tools of its cultivation. I would never have understood the aftermath or human dynamics of farming if I had not visited. As with earlier pilgrimages and *matsuri,* the adventure is almost transcendental, forging a true connection to the local population and land practices. I would never have appreciated snow management—the ballad of snow's drift and the features of its formation. Many of the installations ferret art out of such difficult circumstances, exposing unexpected beauty and chronicling untold stories. I remember Kōbō Abe's 1964 novel *The Woman in the Dunes* and the unabated forces of

Above: MVRDV's Matsudai Snow-land Agrarian Culture Center NOHBUTAI. The large structure withstands the abundant snow. Built next to the train station, the center provides spaces for exhibitions and features a restaurant and store.

Left: Hyogo Art Museum and the Earthquake Memorial Museum, part of the Happy Active Town built after the earthquake of 1995. This art museum has a small collection but vast galleries that are largely empty of people and art. Photo by author, 2013.

Bottom left: *Relation—Blackboard Classroom* is both an exhibition of a prewar classroom and a class for visiting groups. The desks' drawers reveal collections of natural specimens.

Above: *The Rice Field* by Ilya and Emilia Kabakov frames the encounter for the triennial's visitors.

Left and oppposite page: *Harvest House* (left, with architect Kunio Kudo, and opposite top) and *Rice Talk* (opposite bottom) are examples of installations that derive art from cultivation. Part science, part art, the products are enlightening, beautiful, and ephemeral.

The Echigo-Matsunoyama Museum of Natural Science, Kyororo, by Tezuka Architects is a Corten snake withstanding the forces of the snow during the winter.

nature that threaten survival.²¹ Here, art trumps disaster for the moment. The extraordinary Echigo-Matsunoyama Museum of Natural Science, Kyororo, by Tezuka Architects, a Corten snake, stands as a barrier to the blizzard forces and accommodates a snow tunnel with a lantern head, beckoning.

Perhaps the installations in abandoned buildings are the most arresting. They manage to escape the "double nostalgia" of the *furusato*. The loss of a critical mass of population is very real, and in Christian Boltanski and Jean Kalman's *The Last Class* (2006–ongoing), traditional Japanese ghost stories coalesce. Spirits flicker like fireflies in the dark shelter of the school, and I catch glimpses of past assemblies. *Shedding House* (2006–ongoing) by Junichi Kurakake and Nihon University College of Art sculpture students, Haruki Takahashi's *Landscape Creeper* (2009), and Chisen Furukawa's *Family Tree Breathing* (2006) whisper the secret life and death of these houses. *Shedding House*, a lifeless shell more than two hundred years old, has been stripped by student artists, who worked on it for a total of two and a half years. The wood shavings became a resurrected doppelgänger house.

The past is the guide to interpreting the future of these wasted by-products. In Naoshima in the Seto Islands, the fishing village still supports a co-op store and several residences, and also hosts a number of art happenings. Wandering through this still-functioning village, I encounter a half-submerged house/boat floating in an abandoned rice paddy. I glimpse the reflection of the embryo of the future town. These festivals have enlisted landscapes, houses, and villages in a celebration of locality and specificity. Such artful insertions offer insights and commentaries on time and place that can only be found in the recesses of Japan. As a tourist and art pilgrim, I am required to slow down and reconsider juxtapositions and propositions of landscape and art.²² I call upon all of my resources to navigate these unknown territories. I use the ukiyo-e prints of Hiroshige, transfigured to curate a mined landscape. I apply the lessons of novels to follow the fragile underpinnings of new communities and dying institutions. Most importantly, I recognize the fluidity of a Japanese time and space and comprehend how these art festivals build new identities while capitalizing on past traditions. In touring these once-inaccessible enclaves, I discover what has always been and glimpse what it may become.

Opposite: Christian Boltanski and Jean Kalman's *The Last Class* (2006–ongoing)
Above: The island town of Naoshima

Notes

1 During the Edo period, individuals were required to carry a passport and get approval for travel; there were no restrictions, however, on travel to the Ise Shrine. In 1635, a law was passed forbidding foreign travel for Japanese individuals. There are several well known cases in which individuals attempting to leave the country without permission were discovered and put to death. In 1869, the imperial government abolished the *sekisho* (barriers and checkpoints) and individuals became free to travel. The 1873 Land Tax Reform ended feudalism and subjects' mandated places of residence, further facilitating migration, immigration, and travel.

—

2 I found especially interesting the discussion in John Tribe, ed., *Philosophical Issues in Tourism* (Bristol, UK: Channel View Publications, 2009), 43–61. The essay by Alexandre Panouso Netto, "What is Tourism: Definitions, Theoretical Phases and Principles," was helpful in summarizing the contemporary academic discussions of tourism.

—

3 In *The Wind-Up Bird Chronicle* (1994), the main character sits for days in Shinjuku station to discover a critical path. *Underground: The Tokyo Gas Attack and the Japanese Psyche* (1997), a book about the symbolically devastating subway attack, records the systemic trauma and spiritual vacuum that the Aum Shinrikyo cult claimed to address.

4 Penny Fowler, *Frank Lloyd Wright: Graphic Artist* (Rohnert Park, CA: Pomegranate Communications, 2002), 30.

—

5 Jennifer Robinson, "It Takes a Village: Internationalization and Nostalgia in Postwar Japan," in *Mirror of Modernity: Invented Traditions of Modern Japan*, ed. Stephen Vlastos (Berkeley: University of California Press, 1998), 113.

—

6 *Matsuri* exist in cities as well; they are distributed throughout the nation.

—

7 The second chapter of this very important book, "Western Structure Versus Japanese Space," explains these complicated distinctions in detail. Arata Isozaki, *Japan-ness in Architecture* (Cambridge, Mass: MIT Press, 2006).

8 I worked in Isozaki's office on a Luce Fellowship, and my first task was to work on the catalog and the adaptation of *Ma: Space-Time in Japan* for its subsequent venues: the Cooper-Hewitt, Smithsonian Design Museum in New York and the Berkeley Art Museum. These are my recollections from this period.

—

9 At the same time, Isozaki recognized that the Japanese had to be educated in traditional arts. He designed a kimono school in Tokyo, soon after, to teach a generation of women who no longer knew how to wear a kimono and wanted to dress their daughters. This loss of familiarity with traditional culture is a recurring theme for Isozaki.

—

10 Ozu's outstanding films include *Tokyo Story* (1953), *Floating Weeds* (1959), and *Early Summer* (1951). He was known for his unusual style of cinematography, with the camera stationary and positioned at the level of the tatami mat. His subject matter was domestic: the lives of everyday people.

—

11 This is a strategy in traditional garden design of framing views to the outside.

—

12 Arata Isozaki in *Japanese Architect* no. 9 (Summer 1993). This was brought to my attention by Ruth Mandl, GSAPP student.

—

13 Ari Seligmann, "Artpolis Legacies: Proliferation of Public Architecture Programs for Urban Regeneration in Turn-of-the-Century Japan," *Proceedings of the Society of Architectural Historians*, 30th Annual Conference, Australia and New Zealand, July 2–5, 2013. Thanks to Adrian Favell for bringing this essay to my attention.

—

14 Information gathered from the *Satoyama-Satoumi Ecosystems and Human Well-Being: Socio-Ecological Production of Landscapes of Japan*, eds. Anantha Kumar Duraiappah and Koji Nakamura (UN Publication, 2012). Kunio Kudo and Maiko Nishi introduced me to this comprehensive study.

—

15 The Japanese colonized Hokkaido Island after the Meiji Restoration. The Ainu were the resident indigenous people. American consultants assisted the Japanese in developing a dairy industry and beer production facilities. Several buildings, including the clock tower in downtown Sapporo, are modeled after American architecture.

16 Robinson, "It Takes a Village," 118.

—

17 In "Touring Japan-as-Museum: Nippon and Other
    Japanese Imperialist Travelogues," *Positions* 8, no. 3
    (2000), Gennifer Weisenfeld discusses tourism
    in Japan from 1934–41 as an "integral component of
    international relations, designed to facilitate cross-
    cultural understanding." She goes on to argue that
    tourism in the Japanese state sanctioned invitation
    to Westerners to "colonize the country through a kind
    of touristic gaze." This represented one moment in the
    complex negotiation of national identity and tourism.

—

18 Sharon Zukin, *The Cultures of Cities* (Cambridge, MA:
    Blackwell, 1995).

—

19 Williams develops these concepts in several essays and
    his 1958 book *Culture and Society*. His Marxist readings
    of culture were highly influential in the late 1960s and
    1970s, when Kitagawa was a student.

—

20 I am reminded of Hiroshige's depictions of laborers on
    the highway in *53 Stations of the Tokaido*.

—

21 The novel (and the 1964 filmed version by Hiroshi
    Teshigahara) tells the story of an amateur entomologist
    from Tokyo who is stranded in a remote area and
    spends the night with a young woman who lives at
    the bottom of a sand dune. To survive, she is forced
    to shovel the sand that accumulates each day. Western
    science thus confronts primal nature.

—

22 In his essay in this volume, Fram Kitagawa discusses his
    intention of a slow touristic experience.

Afterword: Reflections on the First Five Editions

First Triennial: Learning from Criticism

Criticism from Locals

The first triennial began by pushing past strong opposition. Many people gathered for the opening, but there were fewer visitors thereafter, and although I knew that events such as this tend to receive more visitors during the second half, I was very concerned about attendance. Yet as the time of the Obon festival season neared, people began to arrive, and during the final week there was continuous foot traffic and traffic jams from the more than 160,000 visitors. The triennial was regarded as a new model within the art world in terms of regional development, public works, and networking.

I was still exposed to harsh criticism from some of the locals, the biggest complaint being that there was hardly any participation on their part. Another criticism stemmed from the fact that "art as revitalization" was still an unfamiliar concept. The third criticism was that everything must be costing too much. People also wanted greater transparency regarding how much the artists were paid.

In fact, the only two communities that had been *willing* to participate were Hachi and Gejo, and their workshop participation approximated about three thousand people. This was 4 percent of the total population. And it was to be expected that people would be unfamiliar with art as an agent to revitalize community, since they had never seen it in action before. We were setting a precedent for art and *machizukuri*. The mayors of the six municipalities declared their new intent to explore the boom of "community building through art." An example of the spending of one municipality during three years was 17,460,000 yen (approximately 150,000 dollars). The cost of the thirteen works installed there was 1,340,000 yen (approximately 11,000 dollars) for each piece. It is understood in a region where 5 percent of revenue goes to snow and ice control that this amount of money is important, but these prices are incredibly reasonable in any context. Sixty percent of the total festival budget was covered by the prefecture, funds for road and river public works, and corporate sponsorships. The festival was also made possible by the volunteer work of supporters and residents, as well as artists and specialists. It could be said that the event was unprecedented in terms of cost-effectiveness. With regard to the last question, we maintained that we were not at liberty to disclose the amounts of money that went to the artists.

From "Public Art" to "Site-Specific"

I was in some ways disappointed that the works that stood out were a bit ostentatious—meaning seeming to be coming from outside, and incongruous with their sites. It must have been quite a challenge for some of the artists to produce work in someone else's rice field or home, as opposed to a studio or gallery. But there were also strong works with great potential, such as Ilya and Emilia Kabakov's *Rice Fields*, Oscar Oiwa's *Scarecrow Project*, Marina Abramović's *Dream House*, James Turrell's *House of Light*, Richard Wilson's *Set North for Japan (74° 33′ 2″)*, and Daniel Buren's *La Musique, La Dance*.

These works were strong because they were created on someone else's land, and the clashes they evoked with the residents came to represent the basis for the triennial. Buren's *La Musique, La Dance* became highly site-specific by effectively embracing the *matsuri* festivity in the streets of Tokamachi City. I was impressed that Tokamachi City agreed to display this work, and I hope to revive it someday. I continue to seek artists who understand the Echigo-Tsumari site and can dialogue with local communities.

Guidance to the Artists

Whenever we first meet with artists, I always tell them about Echigo-Tsumari. I explain to them the collapse of the textile industry, the abandoned rice terraces, the shrinking population, the empty houses. My point is not about how tasty the wild vegetables are here or how beautiful the landscape is, but rather about making them aware of the history of regional decline. I explain this context because I want them to use it as a starting point for their works.

One of the best of the *akiya* projects has been Abramović's *Dream House,* which was inaugurated during the first edition of the triennial. The use of closed schools wasn't part of my concept at the beginning; its true implications emerged with Yoshio Kitayama's *To the Dead, to the Living,* which also began in 2000 and led to other closed-school projects. Above all, these pieces give the sense of forging temporality, leaving a strong and lasting impression.

I wasn't necessarily thinking of the triennial as a "festival," nor was I aware of its potentially carnivalesque qualities (although these too became apparent over time).

I was only focused on trying to make certain that each individual piece was interesting enough to allow the triennial to continue. I felt strongly that the departure point needed to be the catalytic reaction between site, building, and artwork.

Discovery of the Journey

The first triennial featured 148 artists from thirty-two countries spread out across the Echigo-Tsumari region. There was criticism about how far apart the works were and people argued that it should be centralized in a smaller area. But part of the intent was to give visitors a reason to explore the different communities in their search for the works. The common response was, "It's hot, tiring, and inefficient, but refreshing." You sweat as you walk, but you also notice the birds and insects flying about, and the smell of the fresh-cut grass. The thin green stalks of rice gently billow in the breeze in the rice terraces. These are the phenomenological aspects of the Echigo-Tsumari experience. In the evening, you nourish your tired body in the *onsen* hot spring and enjoy the local cuisine with sake while talking about the art you saw that day.

This style of "a journey guided by art" was a great discovery in the first triennial. It developed into "the journey of art is best experienced," which has become a model for current trends at art festivals around the world.

Second Triennial: The Uniqueness Showing Through

Use of Public Works

I selected artists for the second triennial specifically in reaction to my sense that many of the works in the first triennial seemed to be relatively uninteresting public art. Some of the most significant works included *Potemkin* by Casagrande & Rintala Architectural Office and *Step in Plan* by John Körmeling.

It was then that we began to see the uniqueness of the Echigo-Tsumari Art Triennale. James Putnam, former contemporary art curator at the British Museum, wrote:

> The Echigo-Tsumari Art Triennale is refreshingly different in both its agenda and organization. Unlike most other multi-site biennial-type events that take place in major capitals of the world, the geographical focus of this triennial is largely rural and provincial.... The contemporary art world has a tendency

to think that progressive, edgy work can only be generated in major cities, yet the standard of some of the work shown here in attractive landscape and village settings makes us question this view and consider this triennial to be a new model for arts festivals.

As a Place of Education

For the second triennial, twenty-one university seminars were involved in the Matsudai Shopping Street Revitalization Project, and eight university seminars were involved in the Tokamachi arcade revitalization efforts. Student involvement has continued throughout the years, and activities take place even when the triennial is not in session. These activities are part of the art and architecture curriculum at many of these universities and have expanded to foreign universities as well.

Echigo-Tsumari is a place for high-impact learning, and it provides multiple modalities of educational engagement.

Third Triennial: Turning Point

Disaster Relief Efforts

The Chūetsu Earthquake struck on October 23, 2004, one year after the second triennial, just when we were building momentum toward preparing for the third. We decided to immediately redirect our efforts to helping with disaster relief. This lasted a year and consisted of the following:

- Weekdays were used to take orders from each community in accordance with the local resident staff.
- Saturdays and Sundays, support "troops" of volunteers from the metropolitan area joined in to help the core local group. Based on the requests of survivors, teams of demolition workers, cleaners, and counselors were formed. The troops from the metropolitan area were small groups so that they could more easily arrive by car in convoys; buses could not access many communities.
- Some supporters wanted to assist in the form of donations, which were often used to buy essential appliances, for instance, washing machines and dryers, large refrigerators, and large-screen TVs. These items were of great help and comfort to people in the shelters.

- Since the local residents now recognized us due to our prior contact with them, they trusted us with the retrieval and handling of their important belongings. Simply by talking with familiar faces, the elderly residents were helped in the healing process.

The disaster relief efforts involved a smooth coordination of the local, the regional, and the metropolitan. These circumstances were also an arena for architects to deploy their skills in demolishing houses, or fixing homes that were partially collapsed.

Artists and other professionals coordinated workshops for local children, who benefited from extracurricular lessons with children from the city who came with their parents who were assisting with disaster relief.

The relationships we built and the trust we gained from the communities during this time directly led to fifty new *akiya* projects in the third triennial. The locals were finally opening their doors to us naturally.

In fall 2005, in response to the locals' desires, we decided to restart preparations for the next triennial, which by then was less than a year away.

Reactions of the Art World

From the beginning, I had no expectations regarding the responses of critics. The first triennial went largely unnoticed by the art world except for the Japanese art critic Yusuke Nakahara, who grasped its meaning from the start. He witnessed the development of the triennial and contributed texts for each of the catalogs, with the following titles: "Leaving the City Behind: Artistic Energy" for the first triennial, "Portents of Restoration in the Arts" for the second, "A Celebration of 'Preart'" for the third, and "What the Echigo-Tsumari Art Triennale Has Brought About" for the fourth. In March 2011, he passed away and his family donated his collection of twenty thousand books to Echigo-Tsumari as the work *Cosmology of Yusuke Nakahara,* which was installed by the artist Tadashi Kawamata in the fifth triennial.

The Tsumari model was finally becoming known at this point as a new method of community development through art, and it captured the attention of curators, museums, and nongovernmental organizations in the West and Asia through international conferences and symposiums. The model indeed translates to various contexts. Echigo-Tsumari received a visit from officials from Nantes, France, a city known for its embrace of creativity. Asian cities such as Beijing, Shanghai, Hong Kong, Seoul, and Taipei are actively exploring *machizukuri* through an emphasis on culture. Obviously, cities need to change and transform as much as rural areas do.

It was during the third edition that many people began to recognize the Echigo-Tsumari Art Triennale as unique in many ways. I began to receive accolades as the director. This was not the result of a marketing plan; I was fueled by my own methodologies, which were built from the ground up, with the passion of the people motivated by *matsuri*-style grassroots efforts.

Fourth Triennial: Ten-Year Anniversary

Toward Economic Sustainability

Grants, sponsorships, and donations had helped pay for the triennial since the beginning. But support from the New Niigata Risou Plan ended in 2006. It was time to lay the foundation for a more self-sustaining model that would not rely so much on the government. The locals, artists, and supporters were in favor of continuing the triennial, but we wouldn't have the funds that were previously subsidized by the prefecture. We invited Hirohiko Izumida, Niigata Prefecture governor, to become a member of our executive committee and to assist us with obtaining grants, foundation funding, and subsidies from national ministries.

Soichiro Fukutake, a well-known art collector and founder and chairman of the Benesse Corporation, had attended the second triennial and offered his cooperation for the third triennial in the form of corporate sponsorship, which we referred to as O-hebi Fukutake Committee (*o-hebi* means "big snake," as opposed to *kohebi*, which means "little snake"). For the fourth edition, he officially became the producer of the Echigo-Tsumari Art Triennale and brought in funding through the so-called *furusato* hometown tax and CSR (Corporate Social Responsibility) activities of corporations and organizations. The *furusato* lets taxpayers allocate some of their taxes to the towns they like and thereby receive a tax deduction. Fukutake explains, "The economy should be a servant to culture" and reflects that his own art activities on Naoshima Island, where he established the Benessee Art Site Naoshima, were greatly informed by his involvement with the triennial. In the catalog for the third edition, Fukutake states, "Using what has existed to create what is to be," and combining "original landscape, contemporary art, and the smiles of the elders of the region are the methods for regional revitalization. My hypothesis was verified in my involvement with Echigo-Tsumari." He continues, "The greatest potential of Japan's revitalization is represented in Naoshima in the west, Tsumari in the east, *satoumi* (village and sea) and *satoyama* (village and mountain)."

Just before the beginning of the third triennial, in July 2006, the Tsumari Fan Club was established. And after the end of the third triennial, a program for the adoption of ownerless terraced rice fields was launched.

Branding of Echigo-Tsumari

The activities in the years between editions have grown since the fourth. Establishing the NPO Echigo-Tsumari Satoyama Collaborative Organization was one significant step. We began to refer to Tokamachi City and Tsunan Town's three hundred square miles as the Echigo-Tsumari Art Field. The branding and networking of people and artworks, along with the *akiya* and closed-school projects, needed to be named in order to be valued as assets to sustain the region by continuing the mission of "using what has existed to create what is to be."

Visitors enjoy the delicious local cuisine of wild vegetables, rice, and mushrooms, and we expanded our local production to generate a real industry. We now have food facilities such as the Matsudai Satoyama Restaurant at the NOHBUTAI, *Ubusuna House,* Hachi Cafe, and the Echigo-Shinanogawa Bal. Lodging options include *Dream House, Shedding House, Sansho House,* and Katakuri Lodge. These all create paid work opportunities for the local residents. There are four hundred people employed during the triennial and one hundred people working in the triennial-related facilities. I monitor these figures closely because they reflect the growth of the region.

The triennial has always resulted in new products by participating artists and the Kohebi Volunteers, and a Roots Echigo-Tsumari Local Product Redesign Project was formally started in the fourth triennial. Through an Internet competition designers were encouraged to submit packaging designs for local products, and the winners were then connected with the (local) makers, resulting in interesting design collaborations. The products have been popular, and some have even received awards outside of Japan. Sales exceeded 85 million yen (approximately 700,000 dollars) during the fourth triennial and 120 million yen (approximately one million dollars) in the fifth.

Maintenance

The triennial has resulted in more than two hundred permanent art installations. There are always problems with the cost and maintenance of outdoor artworks in Tokamachi City and Tsunan Town, given the heavy snowfall. But maintenance work has provided new jobs for the residents.

Kenji Shimotori's *Records of Memory, The People of Ashidaki* (2006–12) is one of the permanent installations, composed of silhouetted representations of actual residents of the community. The individual pieces can be moved, and the maintenance cost is relatively low. The details of the people are so expressively captured that the work is popular among the local residents, and they requested that it be reinstalled after the third triennial. This work serves as a model for considering the maintenance of future works.

Summers and Winters

Echigo-Tsumari is under snow for half the year, and I have been thinking about ways to take advantage of that. Rather than desiring what it doesn't have, a community should try to enhance its local identity and find its universality from there. With that in mind, the community should have ways to play, learn, and think during winter.

In January 2008, the Echigo-Tsumari Snow Art Project started. There have been tours, and artists have been coming to the area to experience the Lunar New Year traditions and participate in enlivening village events.

After years alone in the Gogo-an, a hermitage on Kunigami Mountain, the famous Echigo monk Ryokan developed his philosophy, and, in anticipation of spring, he beautifully expressed a song of impermanence. Learning from him, we also wanted to find a way to work hard during the summer days and then study, read, and think in the winter. In other words, we work hard during the summer days and study when it snows. Starting with the Global Environment Seminar in 2000, we have organized various seminars and workshops to cultivate this connection to working in the summer and studying in the winter.

Fifth Triennial: A Brand-New Stage

Adopted as the Municipal Measure

After the completion of the fourth triennial, the Art Triennale Council was established. Members include Niigata Prefecture and regional organizations, NPO Echigo-Tsumari Satoyama Collaborative Organization, the local community *machizukuri* organization, and scholars. The council held five meetings and sent a proposal to the mayors of Tokamachi City and Tsunan Town. The proposal acknowledged that although the triennial aimed at revitalizing the region and connecting itself to community building, it depended on outside support:

> After the fourth triennial, we have finally seen a significant increase in attention from the world and also participation from the various communities. We are at a crucial moment when we must organize an Echigo-Tsumari brand that can capitalize on this increased attention. We plan to propose how to respond to the challenges of the growing interest in the Echigo-Tsumari Art Triennale. Facing the fifth edition, we are at a crucial moment when we must do further community building through the triennial in response to the support from the outside. The most important problem is how the municipality takes initiative to involve the residents.

The proposal outlined several issues: 1) the triennial as a whole (planning, publicity, administration); 2) the triennial and communities (promotion of existing artworks, community participation, vacant houses and closed schools, use of rice terraces); 3) the triennial and industries, agriculture, tourism (development of special regional products, secondary transportation, accommodation, promotion, linking facilities); and 4) the executive committee (organization, budget, financing).

In response to this recommendation, Yoshifumi Sekiguchi, the mayor of Tokamachi City, decided to prominently position the triennial as one of the central measures of the city. This support came in the event's fifteenth year. Governmental involvement in the triennial is extremely important. But going beyond private sectors to try to establish public activities using taxes raised questions and opposition, and these issues led us to clarify our limitations. Working with people of different positions brings about interesting and dynamic results.

On the one hand, I make demands of the government. To me, unless we eat rice and spend time and effort together, we can't do interesting things. Even if it is inefficient, we should do what is necessary to make a festival, which is not an extension of our daily lives. I'm not here to argue for something frivolous. I am fighting for the existence of the triennial from the standpoint of dire urgency, and I cannot allow myself to retreat from this crucial space for dialogue.

I expect this same intensity from those in the government. This expectation is not always met, which often leads to conflict, but I want us to earnestly consider these issues together. I don't want formalities or niceties; I want results that come from serious reflection and consideration toward a real goal.

Beyond the Disaster

In 2011 there was heavy snow at the beginning of the year, the Northern Nagano Earthquake on March 12, and heavy rains in Niigata and Fukushima at the end of July. The three natural disasters experienced in Echigo-Tsumari hardly deterred the residents from holding the fifth triennial; rather, they still avidly looked forward to it.

The earthquake made me reflect on the severity of the natural elements in the Echigo-Tsumari region. Historically, the area has taken in people who are expelled from other places on political, economic, religious, or cultural grounds, and they survived through their admirable efforts to grow rice here. This has been the pride of the mountain communities of Echigo-Tsumari and an integral part of their identity. In response to the devastation, I felt even more strongly that I would like Echigo-Tsumari to be an accepting, diverse place where anyone can coexist.

Niigata is adjacent to Fukushima Prefecture, and we wanted to create an open-air camp school for children who were evacuees from the disasters in Fukushima. Since 2007, there has been a program there called Children's Summer Camp focused on *satoyama*, communities, and art, and that program was transitioned to support displaced children alongside children from the metropolitan and local areas. This program continues to support victims and families in the *satoyama* landscape through interaction and smiles among all kinds of people. This is not simply a disaster relief effort, but a means of cultivating strong connections to Tohoku.

Museum of Echigo-Tsumari: The Entirety of Echigo-Tsumari

The fifth triennial was marked by the renovation of the Echigo-Tsumari Exchange Center into the Echigo-Tsumari Satoyama Museum of Contemporary Art, KINARE. It was intended to be a microcosm and gateway to the Art Field, with the entire region acting as a museum of *satoyama*.

Originally, Echigo-Tsumari was a place where human activities were in harmony with nature. This is reflected in the "stages," which highlight its various characteristics: heavy snow, the Shinano River, Jomon ruins, beech trees, rice terraces, *se-gae* and *mabu* agricultural methods, civil engineering, roadside gardens, *onsen* hot springs, and mountain vegetables and mushrooms. There are more than thirty permanent *akiya* and closed-schoolhouse projects that serve as the basis for community development, where international architecture and artworks exist, to which the Tokamachi City Museum, the Tokamachi Library, and the Tsunan Town Museum of History and Folklore were added. These works of art and architecture connect the two hundred-plus communities throughout the region. The fifth triennial focused on the idea

of the "Land of Humans" so that visitors could experience the notion that
the Echigo-Tsumari region embodies the connection between people and the
natural environment.

Partnering with the Setouchi Triennale

The Setouchi Art Festival (renamed "Setouchi Triennale" in 2013) was founded in
2010. Soichiro Fukutake served as a general producer, and I was the general director.
Since that time, he and I have worked together in these roles, leading to a partnership
between the two organizations. The Setouchi Art Festival staff shadowed the staff at
the Echigo-Tsumari Art Triennale in the summer of 2009 to gain experience, and
many of the Kohebi Volunteers assisted the Koebi ("little shrimp") Volunteers for
the 2010 Setouchi Art Festival. The Hong Kong University students and graduates
who served as Kohebi Volunteers in the third triennial became involved as artists in
the Setouchi Art Festival, along with some other former Kohebi Volunteers from
abroad who transitioned to become Koebi Volunteers. There are a number of artists
who are involved in both Echigo-Tsumari and Setouchi, as well as audiences who
attend both. There is a synergistic effect from the collaboration, which has certainly
increased visitorship to the triennial.

In this era of globalization, not only foreign tourists and workers travel around the
world, but also those who cherish physical experiences, including artists, performers,
art organizers, and art audiences. These are people who intuitively desire to be
connected with nature and other cultures. This desire evokes the journey of *Homo
sapiens* to unknown lands before the dawn of civilization. This intent is shared by
Setouchi and other regions and will continue to develop connections.

Toward the Future

I feel as though we are embarking on another stage after completing the fifth triennial.
The problems of amassing permanent works and managing their maintenance will
likely lead us to a stricter jurying process. Over the course of the Echigo-Tsumari Art
Triennale, we have developed hotel accommodations, a food and restaurant industry,
and the Kohebi Volunteers. At the same time, we have struggled with regard to the
government, finances, the art world, bureaucracy, and so on. I admit that it has been
an uphill battle, with constant opposition and failures, but we've fought back with
persistence, determined to make improvements. This is how community revitalization

is achieved. Existing social and political systems are inevitable consequences of history, but other parallel forms of society can be imagined. To explore and establish new possibilities, we must struggle with existing realities.

At the time of writing, I'm in the process of preparing for the sixth triennial. There are now 200 permanent works installed. We will continue 23 works shown in previous triennials and produce 124 new works. In addition, there will be 30 events and 4 symposiums, and we will renew 3 school projects. An agricultural training project involving middle-school students from Hong Kong and the Asia Art Platform projects will connect Asian foundations and institutions; the increasing scale and content of this art triennial is starting to match that of the World Expo.

The Echigo-Tsumari region has become healthier and more spirited since we began fifteen years ago. Perhaps we've embarked on a deep and radical undertaking. Besides the Kohebi Volunteers, many thoughtful researchers and successful businesspeople have been involved. But most notable in our efforts have been the blood and sweat of the village communities. Each of the projects at Echigo-Tsumari is informed by the place; the individual artists' significant efforts and their time spent developing relationships become a model for our future. As the organizers of the festival, we are mediators, working behind the scenes without being exclusive. We have to know how people feel about the place they live. I want to lead people to that feeling.

Contributors

Author

Following his graduation from Tokyo National University of Fine Arts and Music (majoring in the history of Buddhist sculpture), Fram Kitagawa organized various exhibitions that introduced to Japan works of art that at the time were not well known. He has been responsible for a wide range of projects, such as the 1978–79 Antoni Gaudí exhibition, which traveled to thirteen Japanese cities, and the *Apartheid Non! International Art Festival* (1988-90), which traveled to 194 venues throughout Japan. Kitagawa has received high praise for his involvement in activities related to community development, such as his lead role in the planning of the Faret Tachikawa Art Project and the cultural activities he oversees at the Daikanyama Hillside Terrace, which was awarded the Mécénat Grand Prix.

He served as the general director of the Echigo-Tsumari Art Triennale in 2000, 2003, 2006, 2009, 2012, and 2015, and has made a major contribution to the development of the region through art. He has served as the general director of the Setouchi Triennale since 2010.

Kitagawa, who is the chairman of Art Front Gallery, is the recipient of many awards, including the Ordre des Arts et des Lettres from the French Republic, the Order of Culture from the Republic of Poland, the 2006 Japanese Education Minister's Award for Art (in the field of art promotion), and the Order of Australia: Honorary Member (AO) in the General Division (2012).

Amiko Matsuo teaches ceramics at California State University, Channel Islands. Her ceramic art investigates identity and the notion of invented traditions and cross-cultural exchanges occurring throughout ceramic history. Her current endeavors involve a series of ceramic works fired with a dusting of ash gathered from local fires to emphasize the cyclical nature of fire in Southern California and to reference the ash glazes in Echizen ware. As a collaborative project at the intersection of artistic and ecological processes, some of these pieces are ritually "chaparral fired" in Southern California landscapes through the help of local firefighters. See her work at amikomatsuoceramics.com.

Brad Monsma's book *The Sespe Wild: Southern California's Last Free River* (2007) explores the environmental and cultural history of Sespe Creek, its endangered species, and its management dilemmas. Often exploring the calibration between human memory and environmental history, his writings have appeared in *Surfer's Journal, Pilgrimage, ISLE, High Country News,* and numerous anthologies. His ceramic work has appeared in juried exhibitions. He is a professor of English at California State University, Channel Islands.

Essayists

Adrian Favell is chair in sociology and social theory at the University of Leeds, England. A 2006–7 Japan Foundation Abe Fellow, he is the author of *Before and After Superflat: A Short History of Japanese Contemporary Art, 1990–2011* (2012) and has also published essays in *Art in America, Bijutsu Techo, Impressions, Artforum,* and *ART-iT online*. He is currently working on a book about postgrowth art and architecture in Japan with Julian Worrall.

Lynne Breslin is a practicing architect based in New York City. She holds an AB from Harvard University and received a MArch and MA from Princeton University. She was a Luce scholar working in Tokyo for the Isozaki Atelier in the late 1970s. Her built projects include award-winning residences, institutional buildings, and exhibition designs for major museums. She has created exhibits for the U.S. Holocaust Museum in Washington, D.C., the Bonsai Museum at the Brooklyn Botanic Gardens, the Whitney Museum, Nelson Atkins Gallery, the New-York Historical Society, and the Empire State Building, among others. She has taught history, theory, and design at Columbia Graduate School of Architecture, Preservation and Planning since 1986.

Index

Acknowledgments

I want to express my deep appreciation and thanks to everyone involved in the Echigo-Tsumari Art Triennale, including the artists, the administrators and organizers, the Kohebi Volunteers, and the village communities. I particularly thank Amiko Matsuo, Brad Monsma, Kevin Lippert, Jennifer Lippert, Nicola Brower, Kunio Kudo, and Rei Maeda for their help.

Fram Kitagawa, May 2015

Photo Credits

(Credits are listed by image number if not otherwise noted.)

Yuji Abe: 033–035

Daici Ano: 061

Anzai: page 47, page 195, 001–002, 004, 008, 010–014, 017–018, 020–024, 031–032, 056–057, 063–069, 073–075, 091, 107, 111, 113, 118–19, 123, 125, 130, 142–49, 151–66, 168–70, 173–74, 178, 200, 204–207, 211

Shigeru Aoyagi: 029

Brett Boardman: 209

Shigemitsu Ebie: 095

Arnold Groeschel: 121

Tadamasa Iguchi: 083

Masanori Ikeda: 050, 058, 060, 062, 085

Kang Chulgyu: 179

Yukiko Kataoka: 198

Kazue Kawase: 055, 079, 124, 181, 184

T. Kobayashi: 098, 116, 122, 167

T. Kuratani: 014, 053, 059, 070, 120, 126

Takenori Miyamoto: 016, 025, 030, 033, 037–038, 051, 071, 084, 086–090, 092–094, 096–097, 099–101, 115, 150, 175–76, 180, 182, 187, 189, 197, 202–203, 208

Hitoshi Miyata: 196

Daido Moriyama: 039–040, 185

Isamu Murai: 019

Osamu Nakamura: pages 1–3, page 139 (traditional event), 003, 005–006, 009, 026–028, 036, 041–049, 052, 072, 081, 105, 108, 127–29, 131–41, 172, 177, 183, 186, 190, 195, 199, 201, 210

Hiroshi Noguchi: 102, 104

Hisao Ogose: 054, 112

Hikaru Sasaki: 076–078

All other photos were taken by the artists and the organizers of the triennial.

Published by
Princeton Architectural Press
37 East Seventh Street
New York, New York 10003

Visit our website at www.papress.com

Originally published by Gendaikikakushitsu Publishers under the title
美術は地域をひらく: 大地の芸術祭10の思想
© 2014 Fram Kitagawa and Gendaikikakushitsu Publishers

This publication would not have been possible without the generous support of the
Japan Foundation.

国際交流基金

English edition
© 2015 Princeton Architectural Press
All rights reserved
Printed and bound in China
18 17 16 15 4 3 2 1 First edition

Editor: Nicola Brower
Layout and typesetting: MaryAnn George

Special thanks to: Janet Behning, Erin Cain, Megan Carey, Carina Cha, Tom Cho, Barbara Darko,
Benjamin English, Russell Fernandez, Jan Cigliano Hartman, Jan Haux, Mia Johnson,
Diane Levinson, Jennifer Lippert, Katharine Myers, Jaime Nelson, Rob Shaeffer, Sara Stemen,
Marielle Suba, Kaymar Thomas, Paul Wagner, Joseph Weston, and Janet Wong
of Princeton Architectural Press —Kevin C. Lippert, publisher

Library of Congress
Cataloging-in-Publication Data
Kitagawa, Furamu, 1946–
[Bijutsu wa chiiki o hiraku. English]
Art place Japan : the Echigo-Tsumari Triennale and the vision to reconnect art and nature /
Fram Kitagawa ; Translated by Amiko Matsuo and Brad Monsma ; with essays by Lynne Breslin
and Adrian Favell. — English edition.
        pages   cm
Includes index.
ISBN 978-1-61689-424-5 (paperback)
1. Echigo-Tsumari Art Triennale. 2. Art festivals—Japan—Niigata-ken. 3. Art, Modern—
21st century—Themes, motives. I. Title.
NX430.J32N555 2015
709.52'0905—dc23
                                                    2015017746